THE JOY OF

THE

TRINITY

TARA-LEIGH COBBLE

THE JOY OF
THE
TRINITY

ONE GOD,
THREE PERSONS

B&H
PUBLISHING
BRENTWOOD, TENNESSEE

Published by B&H Publishing Group
Brentwood, Tennessee

Dewey Decimal Classification: 231.044
Subject Heading: TRINITY / CHRISTIANITY—DOCTRINES /
GOD

Cover design by B&H Publishing Group.
Cover image by Aleksandra Konoplya/Alamy.
Author photo by Meshali Mitchell.

1 2 3 4 5 6 7 • 27 26 25 24

For every person who loves God
—even just an ounce—
and wants to love Him more.

Acknowledgments

Lisa Jackson—who saw this book in my heart before I did.
Anne MacDonald—who helped me unearth the joy in it all.
Olivia Le—who holds it all together so I can write.

Contents

Introduction

If you had to describe God's personality, what would you say? Not what He *does* but His demeanor. Not what He's capable of but what He's *like*.

Here's how King David described God: "In your presence there is fullness of joy; at your right hand are pleasures forevermore" (Ps. 16:11). He also said God's presence brings gladness and joy (Ps. 21:6)!

Does it surprise you to know that God is *happy*? He is infinitely joyful! And because He's so delighted, He can be delightful to us—by sharing who He is with us. If joy is your goal, knowing the triune God will be supremely useful to you. In fact, this is the only path to true joy.

But that doesn't mean it will be an easy path. Everything beautiful in life has some level of unavoidable difficulty attached to it, including our best and strongest relationships. In every relationship, you have to go through the process of getting to know that person. Along the way you face misunderstandings and miscommunications; maybe you also encounter unmet expectations—all as a part of building the relationship. People are wonderfully complex, aren't we?

Our relationship with God has a lot of those same complexities because He's a Person too. *Three* Persons, actually— Father, Son, and Spirit. You're likely here because you already agree with the idea of the trinitarian God of the Bible, but you may not know what that means. So, to a certain degree, I'll assume we're on the same page and that I don't need to spend paragraphs or pages convincing you God exists or the Bible is true. However, even those of us who consent to belief in the Trinity have a hard time grasping exactly what (or *Who?*) it is (*They are?*). See how complex it already feels?

J. I. Packer says the doctrine of the Trinity "confronts us with perhaps the most difficult thought that the human mind has ever been asked to handle. It is not easy; but it is true."[1] Someone once said, "If you don't believe in the Trinity, you will lose your soul. But if you try to understand it, you will lose your mind."[2] It's true that some things are beyond our *complete* knowledge, but they aren't beyond our *partial* knowledge. So in this book, we'll make it our aim to know the highest percentage of what our minds can possibly grasp. After all, knowing Him is the path to joy, and I want *as much joy as possible.*

I was born with several birth defects, mostly related to my heart. I remember having surgeries as a kid, and the doctors would say, "You're going to take a little nap, and when you wake up, we'll give you ice cream!" Seriously? Deal! Naps and ice cream are my love languages! But now I know it was *more* than just a nap. Back then, I experienced the blessings of anesthesia without knowing its name or being able to explain it. But even after I learned the word "anesthesia," I still didn't understand it.

In 2016, I had two open-heart surgeries to fix those birth defects. During that process, I became friends with one of my ICU nurses who eventually quit that job and began working to become a nurse anesthetist. According to her, no one fully understands what anesthesia is or how it works. But she's still paying lots of money to study it so she can work in that field someday.

Anesthesiologists know more than she'll know when she becomes a nurse anesthetist. And she knows more than I know. And I know more now than I did as a kid, even being a kid who had experienced the blessing of it personally and whose life had been saved by it. Spending time to better understand the Trinity is similar: it is a mystery to even the most studied professionals, and everyone knows it can't be *fully* understood. But it can be *more* understood by those willing to study it. So while we will never fully understand the Trinity—at least not in this life—we can understand more than we currently do.

And if it leads to fullness of joy (a lot more joy than ice cream, mind you!), why wouldn't we?

———————————

If we know we *can* learn more about the Trinity, and we know that joy is promised on the other side of our learning, then why do people tend to brush over it instead of dig in? What makes this doctrine so challenging?
I believe there are a few things that contribute to our collective confusion and difficulty with the Trinity.

1. Simplified Explanations

If you've ever been part of a Bible study or a Sunday School class that talked about the Trinity, you've likely heard analogies of shamrocks and eggs and H_2O. Maybe someone has drawn a picture of a triangle or a shield. Every analogy of the Trinity breaks down at some level simply because there's nothing else in existence quite like God. Everything else has a point of origin and relies on the things around it for its definition, but God is uncreated and has always been who He is.

Some analogies are better than others, but even those require caveats. Other analogies are downright heretical—which is to say, they tell more of a lie about God than a truth, and they're more harmful than helpful in giving us a right view of God. (See a list of heresies on page 193.) He isn't dependent on anything else to be who He is, so when we compare Him to something that inherently is dependent on something else, it will always lead us down the wrong path. We crave analogies because they seem to help simplify God, and we prefer to simplify Him because it's easier than studying His complexity. But is that how you want to be known? Is that how you aim to build a relationship with anyone you love? Simplified explanations fall short of being enlightening or fulfilling in our relationship with God.

2. Selfishness

This answer may not apply to you, but it certainly does to me. My selfishness was one of the biggest hurdles that kept me from digging into the Trinity. I preferred to focus on God's promises to me and all the things He could do to benefit me, so I was content to stop short of looking for *who He is*. I tuned out when someone mentioned the Trinity—not because I already knew all the details but because I didn't yet know enough. I was in for a real surprise when I did begin to study the Trinity. It isn't just a theological concept; fundamentally, it's a *relationship*. To have a healthy, functioning relationship, you have to look beyond yourself and get to know the other person involved.

3. The Bible Never Uses the Word *Trinity*

However, that doesn't mean the triune God is not addressed in Scripture. In fact, we'll read more Trinity-related passages than you can imagine! The idea of the Trinity is found throughout the Bible, starting in Genesis 1:1. Jesus talked about it in the Gospels, and the apostles affirmed it throughout their New Testament letters. Still, the early church struggled to summarize it until a theologian named Tertullian, who lived about a century after Jesus's resurrection, created the word *Trinity* to succinctly reference Scripture's teaching about God.[3]

(By the way, many books cover how and why and when the early church named and articulated the doctrine of the Trinity as it appears in Scripture. Other books investigate the original words and languages used in Scripture to explain the Trinity. And there are still others that show how the Trinity is unique to Christianity and how our triune God stands in stark contrast to the gods of other religions. We won't cover those topics in-depth, but in case you're interested in learning more about any of them, I've built out a list of suggestions on page 202.)

––––––––––––

This doctrine is absolutely necessary to the Christian faith. Its importance can't be overemphasized. Theologian Ligon Duncan said that asking, *Is the identity of the Trinity important to the gospel?* is similar to asking, "Is who your wife is central to your marriage?"[4] Without the Trinity as the core of our beliefs, every other doctrine of our faith starts to come unglued and unhinged. You cannot have the Christian faith without a triune God. This is a bold statement, but the creeds support it. (See pages 195–199 to read the Athanasian Creed.) Every other Christian belief is built on this foundation. Without it, we slide into the cultic beliefs of Mormons, Jehovah's Witnesses, or Muslims.

It's tempting to diminish the importance of the Trinity and to seek a false peace by simply "focusing on the Word of God." But that's shallow at best and foolish at least. In fact, God's Word is precisely where we learn about His Persons; He's given it to us so we can know Him in greater depth. How heartless and arrogant to want to know less of Him than He has made possible. People who truly know God have always wanted to know God more—both for their own sakes and for the sake of being able to talk more clearly about Him and His love with others. So I'm glad you're here, trying—digging in. And I know God smiles at it too. He loves to be known and understood and loved, just like you love to be known and understood and loved.

By the end of this book, you'll be shocked at the dimension, texture, and beauty you've started to see in the triune God. It has been there all along—in the Bible we read and the songs we sing—but perhaps we're too familiar with it to notice it. Chances are you're already immersed in some level of knowledge or assumption about the Trinity, so you'll find that instead of *starting over* with your beliefs about the Father, Son, and Spirit, you'll likely just *develop* them as we move through this book together. Those beliefs will grow muscles! It will be challenging, but by God's power at work within you, I believe you will know and love Him more than you ever thought possible!

———————

There are three additional things I want to point out before we begin:

1. I've written a Bible study on the same topic—it's called *He's Where the Joy Is: Getting to Know the Captivating God of the Trinity*. Why a book *and* a Bible study? Because the Trinity is so important. It's a classic Christian topic that should be explored not just in one way, but a variety of ways. Each format offers its own approach, depending on the medium you prefer. In my mind, I'd want you to explore both formats (or even give one as a gift to a theologically curious friend), because you really can't get enough of the Trinity!

2. Since we may be covering some terms you aren't familiar with yet, I've included a glossary in the back of the book. Words that appear in the glossary are in bold font, underlined (e.g., **theophany**).

3. You'll also find some additional helps in the back of the book: the Athanasian Creed, a list of heresies, and suggestions for further study on this topic.

1

Unity and Diversity

"The divine nature is really and entirely identical
with each of the three persons, all of whom can
therefore be called one." —Thomas Aquinas[1]

"While the three members of the Trinity are distinct, this
does not mean that any is inferior to the other. Instead, they
are all identical in attributes. They are equal in power,
love, mercy, justice, holiness, knowledge, and all other
qualities. Each Person is fully God." —Matt Perman[2]

As we approach such a complex topic, I want you to know that *you can do this.* You can grow in your understanding of the Trinity in a way that amplifies your love for God and transforms your life. We're going to take it slowly, and I'm going to explain things in common laymen's terms because that's what I am: a layman. I may occassionally use a bigger theological term, but I've aimed to define those in the glossary in the back. (Note: those words will be bolded and underlined.) If you come across a confusing word that is not in the glossary (bolded/underlined), do a web search for the definition.

There are lots of ways we could approach studying the Trinity. This is how I've done it: first, we'll start in this chapter by looking at what God says about Himself—Father, Son, and Spirit. We'll see how they're unified, *and* how they're distinct. In the three chapters that follow, we'll take a look at each Person individually. Then we'll wrap up with two chapters about how this information impacts us—how God's identity informs our relationship with Him and subsequently with the world around us. Everything He is changes everything we are, and it is the most joy-inducing thing I can imagine! I'm excited for us to learn about Him and to watch His beauty unfold all around us.

God's Revealing

Have you ever fumbled through your house in a power outage, bumping into walls and bruising your shins on the coffee table? You easily navigate your way around that furniture on a daily basis, but with the lights off, it can be more of a challenge. Many of us who have spent time in church or in Scripture keep bumping into the Trinity but aren't able to identify or describe it clearly. There's a good reason for that. Through most of the Bible, it may seem as though God doesn't say a lot about the Trinity—at least not directly.

I borrowed the darkened house illustration from B. B. Warfield, who said the Old Testament is like a furnished room that is dimly lit, and the New Testament is where God flips on the light switch.[3] This is especially true where the Trinity is concerned. The Trinity "furniture" has been there all along, sitting in the same spots, and the New Testament light just reveals where the furniture has always been.

It's not as though God was being cruel in the Old Testament. He wasn't trying to bruise any shins. He knows relationships work best through **progressive revelation**, a gradual revealing of more and more information over time. In healthy relationships, we don't expect to share or learn everything the first time we meet someone. This is how Scripture describes God's relationship with humanity. He didn't reveal His whole plan for His people at one time. Instead, He used different means at different times, patiently giving us more information piece by piece as He moved through the process.

Despite God's progressive revelation, you and I have most likely suffered from another problem: we've been living in this furnished, lit house while wearing blindfolds. We've bumped into some things here and there; we've sat on them and trusted their ability to hold us up. Perhaps we've even occasionally gotten a glimpse of the room layout when we tilt our heads at just the right angle. But we haven't actively explored what He progressively revealed. Now is the time for us to take our blindfolds off and let the light of Scripture show us the beauty and design of this house we've been living in.

(Another problem we've suffered is running into false ideas about God's trinitarian nature that were never true of Him to begin with! If you're interested in those, look through the list of heresies on pages 193–194. Make note if you've encountered any of them, or if you've unknowingly and accidentally believed one of them. This list will give you a helpful place to return and review in case you hear something about God that strikes you as odd, wrong, or confusing.)

Much of what we know about the Trinity wasn't revealed until the New Testament. In the Old Testament, God's first priority was explaining to His people that He is ONE God—the one true God. **Polytheism** was rampant among all the other nations, and God wanted to redirect the hearts of His people to the truth, so He repeated this theme throughout the Old Testament. In fact, to both ancient and modern Jews who rely on the Old Testament, the most important Scripture is generally regarded to be Deuteronomy 6:4, "Hear, O Israel: The LORD our God, the LORD is one." God is one. This **doctrine** stands out as the most important doctrine of the Old Testament, the heart of **monotheism** (the belief in one true God—as opposed to polytheism, the belief in many gods). But this verse points to far more than just the fact that there is one true God; it points to His preeminence. He is singular in His essence and superior in His being.

Since the ancient Jews were surrounded by polytheistic nations, the Old Testament writers spent a lot of effort establishing there is one true God. Only then could God begin to introduce more complexity about Himself: He is one God who consists of three Persons. In the next steps of His progressive revelation, God sent His Son to earth to dwell among the people and then sent His Spirit to dwell within His people. Here's how Hebrews 1:1–3 (csb) puts it:

> Long ago God spoke to our ancestors by the prophets at different times and in different ways. In these last days, he has spoken to us by his Son. God has appointed him heir of all things and made the universe through him. The Son is the radiance of God's glory and the exact expression of his nature, sustaining all things by his powerful word. After making purification for sins, he sat down at the right hand of the Majesty on high.

God's process remains obscured to someone who only reads the Old Testament. To see the Trinity in the Old Testament, you have to read it through the New Testament lens. But make no mistake: God had been dropping hints about the Trinity since Genesis 1. We'll see some of them in this book.

There's one important thing we must note when it comes to Scripture's progressive revelation: it is not corrective revelation. When God reveals something new, He doesn't negate something He previously revealed. He builds on and expands what He has already revealed. For instance, read Genesis 1:1–2 and John 1:1–3:

> In the beginning **God** created the heavens and the earth. Now the earth was formless and empty, darkness covered the surface of the watery depths, and the **Spirit of God** was hovering over the surface of the waters. (Gen. 1:1–2 csb, emphasis added)

> In the beginning was the **Word**, and the **Word was with God**, and the **Word was God**. He was with God in the beginning. **All things were created through him**, and apart from him not one thing was created that has been created. (John 1:1–3 csb, emphasis added)

Do you see it? At the start of the world's story, we see hints of the Trinity—God's Spirit and God's Word (whom other Scripture passages identify as God's Son) were the means God used to do His work of creation. God was doing one work—creating the universe—through what we only later come to understand as His three Persons.

And don't forget that mankind is part of the universe that our triune God created. Evidence of the Trinity's presence is as clear in the creation of humans as it is in the creation of the sun, moon, and stars. Just read Genesis 1:26 and notice the "our" language. If you've ever wondered who "our" is in this passage, it's the Trinity!

> Then God said, "Let us make man in **our** image, according to **our** likeness. They will rule the fish of the sea, the birds of the sky, the livestock, the whole earth, and the creatures that crawl on the earth." (CSB, emphasis added)

Look back at the John 1 passage above. Remember that the Bible presents Jesus Christ as the Word of God (John 1:14; Rev. 19:13–16). So when we put the pieces together, we can see that the preincarnate Christ was present in creation, as described in Genesis 1, as was God's Spirit, who "was hovering over the face of the waters" (Gen. 1:2). When the New Testament points to the Spirit, His actions are described with similar fluttering, wind-related words, helping us see He is the same Person who was present and active at creation. The Old and New Testaments work together to help us better understand what God has been saying all along about His presence and activity in our world.

In our journey to know God better, we've now covered the fact that God is a *revealer*. He reveals His nature, a nature that is triune. The next thing we can learn about God to know Him better is to spend some time looking at God's *unity* (as it applies to His oneness) and His *diversity* (as it applies to the three Persons of the Trinity).

God's Unity

As we move through this book, we'll cover the three foundations of the Trinity multiple times so you'll know them by heart when we finish.

The First Foundation of the Trinity Is: There Is Only One True God.

The Bible's descriptions of *Elohim* (the name God gives Himself in Gen. 1:1) and His actions set Him apart from all other gods of all other religions.[4] The Old Testament authors repeatedly emphasized the theme of God's superiority and His oneness. These two themes are tied together: not only is our God the one true God who is set apart in power and eternality, but He is ONE God. If there were any other gods on His level, they would have to be eternal like Him and all-powerful like Him, which is functionally impossible—not only because one of them would've had to create the other but because that would also require one to predate the other.

Consider the passages below. Do you see any words that point to God's oneness and unity? Make note of them as you read.

"Do not have other gods besides me."
(Exod. 20:3 csb)

"Listen, Israel: The Lord our God, the Lord
is one. Love the Lord your God with all your
heart, with all your soul, and with all your
strength."
(Deut. 6:4–5 csb)

"You are my witnesses" . . . and my servant
whom I have chosen, so that you may know
and believe me and understand that I am he.
No god was formed before me, and there will
be none after me."
(Isa. 43:10 csb)

This is what the Lord, your Redeemer who
formed you from the womb, says: I am the
Lord, who made everything; who stretched
out the heavens by myself; who alone spread
out the earth.
(Isa. 44:24 csb)

"Turn to me and be saved,
all the ends of the earth.
For I am God,
and there is no other."
(Isa. 45:22 csb)

Since progressive revelation isn't corrective, the New Testament reiterates the theme of "oneness" from the Old Testament, even as it helps us understand the three Persons of God.

For more clarity from the Scriptures, read the following verses slowly and carefully. Can you see the aspects within these passages that point to God's *unity and oneness*? On the other hand, can you see which aspects point to His *diversity* of Persons?

> Then God said, "Let us make man in our image, according to our likeness. They will rule the fish of the sea, the birds of the sky, the livestock, the whole earth, and the creatures that crawl on the earth."
>
> So God created man
> in his own image;
> he created him in the image of God;
> he created them male and female.
> (Gen. 1:26–27 csb)

> "Go, therefore, and make disciples of all nations, baptizing them in the name of the Father and of the Son and of the Holy Spirit." (Matt. 28:19 csb)

> Yet for us there is one God, the Father. All things are from him, and we exist for him.

And there is one Lord, Jesus Christ. All things
are through him, and we exist through him.
(1 Cor. 8:6 csb)

It's an interesting exercise to see both God's oneness and
His diversity on display in the Bible, isn't it? Here's something
I caught when looking at Matthew 28:19: we are baptized
into only one name (singular), not names (plural)! This is significant, especially as it refers collectively to the three Persons
of God. In Scripture, a name represents the will, character,
and essence of a person. The Trinity has one will, character,
and essence across all three divine Persons, even in the Old
Testament where the Trinity is less evident.

Consistency

If you've ever studied the Old Testament, you may have
come away thinking something along these lines: *Why is God
so angry in the Old Testament? I like the New Testament better.
God is so much nicer after Jesus shows up on the scene.*

I've had those thoughts too. But when we pull God and
His actions out of context, as we're often prone to do, it's easy
to misunderstand His character. If we divide Him into three
Persons without remembering He is ONE, we may begin to
assign certain temperaments to the Persons of the Trinity (i.e.,
the Father is the angry one; Jesus is the nice one, and the
Spirit is the weird and/or mysterious one). The good news for
us (as we will come to see in the pages ahead) is that this is

theologically impossible. Much to our relief, "Old Testament God" isn't unlikable as we may have believed Him to be. For all of us who have ever felt that way, Scripture is here to set us straight and invite us into something much more beautiful and winsome. Whew!

Contrary to popular thought, God doesn't undergo a personality transplant at the end of the Old Testament. When we follow the story line of Scripture, we see a God who created mankind out of an overflow of love, who clothed Adam and Eve before they even repented, who rescued the Israelites out of slavery and then led them as they established a functioning society, joyfully choosing to set up camp in their midst and repeatedly forgiving them, blessing them, and reminding them He was sending a Messiah to rescue them. This is the heart of God evident in the scope of the Old Testament's metanarrative. All along He dropped hints of what was coming, and then He delivered on His promise!

Of course, if we drop down in the middle of the Old Testament in a time when He's punishing the Israelites, He seems harsh. We won't understand why His laws were helpful and necessary. We'll fail to notice He's already told them repeatedly not to do that specific sinful thing, told them what type of punishment to expect if/when they do it, and then continued to provide for them and protect them despite their rebellion. With our limited information, we'll view Him as strict or angry, and we won't draw near to Him. We'll prefer to stay in the New Testament where we can read about Jesus, who paid for all the sins we know we've committed. This is a common problem we encounter when we don't read the story of Scripture chronologically (in the order it happened, not the order it is laid out). Reading the Bible at all is an important endeavor, but reading chronologically can help us get to know God in the order He chose to reveal Himself through progressive revelation.

There is a necessary process of the gospel: we must be confronted with God's laws and requirements, see that we fall short and can't obey His laws, and realize our need for rescue. Jesus came to be that Rescuer. He not only paid our sin debt, but He also granted us His righteousness! This is how progressive revelation works in our relationship with God, and it's the reason we still desperately need the truths of the Old Testament in order to see Him rightly!

The same is true of our understanding of the Trinity. Without the Old Testament, it might be easy to divide God into three separate Gods, or even to think God shape-shifts from one "form" into the other. (See *Tritheism and Modalism* in the list of heresies on pages 193–194.) But when we read Scripture as a whole, we see His oneness throughout, which helps us maintain this doctrinal balance: *Each Person of the Trinity indwells the other two.* We can't emphasize one Person of God over the others. It's vital to view them holistically, or we'll be led into heresy. But the Trinity doesn't mean God is divided into three parts like pieces of a pie. *Each Person of the Trinity fully possesses/is the complete divine essence.* The word we use to describe this is **consubstantial**—regarded as the same in substance or essence.

Since they are all equally and fully divine within the Trinity unto themselves, no one Person plays an eternally dominant role. They each point to the others. The Father glorifies and points to the Son. The Son glorifies and points to the Father and the Spirit, and the Spirit glorifies and points to the Son and the Father. Understanding this truth is VITAL. It shows us so much about God's character. He is always pointing externally—even with Himself. This shows us the heart of God is focused on outgoing love.

The Persons of God aren't only united in their essence, but they're united in their purpose as well. And this divine, eternal unity is inseparable. God has always been One, and He has always been Three. He didn't become this way to serve some kind of purpose or function; it is who He is and how He is.

As we wrap up this section on God's unity and move on to God's diversity, take a moment to pause and etch the first foundation of the Trinity in your mind right now: THERE IS ONLY ONE TRUE GOD.

God's Diversity

The Second Foundation of the Trinity Is: There Are Three Divine Persons of the One True God.

Consider Genesis 1:1:

In the beginning, God created the heavens
and the earth.

If you look up the term *Elohim* (the name God uses for
Himself in this verse) in a Hebrew lexicon, you'd probably be
surprised to find that it is plural, not singular.

In his book *Shared Life*, Donald Macleod said, "The New
Testament disclosure of the Father, the Son, and the Holy
Spirit is the best, and possibly the only, explanation of God's
giving himself a plural name [*Elohim*]" in the Old Testament.[5]

Having a God who is one in nature/being and three in
Persons can seem confusing or contradictory, but that's simply
because there's nothing else like Him in existence. No other
religion in the history of the world has ever had a God like
this, and we would do well to learn about Him since He's the
foundation of our faith.

Not long after God flipped the lights on in the New
Testament, Christians began trying to find ways to summarize
and explain this doctrine. As we discussed in the introduction,
all analogies sacrifice some aspect of who He is and lead us
to one or more heresies we already discussed (see page 4). As
complex as the Trinity may be, you and I benefit personally
from the fact that God is both One and triune. So we won't
simplify His complexity; we'll study it. After all, stained-glass
windows are more captivating because of their many panes
and colors. Diamonds are more brilliant and valuable as their
facets increase. God's complexity adds to His beauty, and
not only does He invite us into His mysteries, but He offers

wisdom if we ask Him (James 1:5), and He shares His secrets with His friends (Ps. 25:14)—and that's you!

The Third Foundation of the Trinity Is: The Three Persons Are Co-Equal, Co-Eternal, and Co-Relational.

God is one essence (or nature) and three Persons: the Father, Son, and Spirit are all equally and fully God, and "the being of each Person is equal to the whole being of God."[6] They're not only equal in character and personality but also in power, glory, and eternality. Since they're all co-eternal, that means none of them were created by the others. This is important, and it's one of the places where our modern, Western mindset often fails us because we're tempted to attach ages to their names.

We think of a father as one who comes before a son and who played a role in creating that son and who must be separate from the son even though they share some DNA. But in the eternal Godhead, the name *Father* points to One who gives His identity to another person; He is the Unbegotten and the Begetter. The "Son" is the One who displays that identity. Hebrews 5:5 describes Jesus as being "begotten" of the Father, which conveys the idea of the Father appointing the Son, not creating Him. To prevent any confusion about this, theologians often use the phrase "eternally begotten" to describe Jesus (John 1:1–18). As for the Spirit, Jesus described Him as the One who "proceeds from" the Father (John 15:26), and there's also evidence He proceeds from the Son (John 16:7).

While we may not understand this fully, Scripture helps us understand it better.

These descriptions of appointing, sending, begetting, and proceeding tell us a lot about the Trinity: they're united in their mission, and they have distinct roles as they engage with us in that mission.

Since they are co-eternal and co-equal Persons on a united mission, it's vital for us to remember that one of them isn't more important than the other. In his book *Forgotten Trinity*, James R. White described it like this: "Just because the Father, Son, and Spirit do different things does not mean that any one of them is inferior to the others in nature. Think of it this way: in eternity past, the Father, Son, and Spirit voluntarily and freely chose the roles they would take in bringing about the redemption of God's people. . . . Each took different roles of necessity."[7]

Consider the following verses. Notice how each bolded word (including nouns and pronouns) refers to a Person of the Trinity. (Note: in these verses, *God* usually refers to the Father.)

> "Go, therefore, and make disciples of all nations, baptizing them in the name of the **Father** and of the **Son** and of the **Holy Spirit**." (Matt. 28:19, emphasis added)

> At that time **[Jesus]** rejoiced in the **Holy Spirit** and said, "I praise you, **Father,** Lord

of heaven and earth, because **you** have hidden these things from the wise and intelligent and revealed them to infants. Yes, **Father,** because this was **your** good pleasure." (Luke 10:21 csb, emphasis added)

Now it is **God** who strengthens us together with you in **Christ,** and who has anointed us. **He** has also put **his** seal on us and given us the **Spirit** in our hearts as a down payment. (2 Cor. 1:21–22 csb, emphasis added)

The grace of the Lord **Jesus Christ,** and the love of **God,** and the fellowship of the **Holy Spirit** be with you all. (2 Cor. 13:13 csb, emphasis added)

For this reason I kneel before the **Father** from whom every family in heaven and on earth is named. I pray that **he** may grant you, according to the riches of **his** glory, to be strengthened with power in your inner being through **his Spirit,** and that **Christ** may dwell in your hearts through faith. I pray that you, being rooted and firmly established in love, may be able to comprehend with all the saints what is the length and width, height and depth of **God's** love, and to know **Christ's** love that

surpasses knowledge, so that you may be filled
with all the fullness of **God**. (Eph. 3:14–19 csb)

It's common to refer to the Persons of God in this order:
the Father is the first Person of God; the Son is the second
Person of God; and the Spirit is the third Person of God. But
it's important to note that this order doesn't mean one Person
is older or more important than the others. Instead, this order
points to God's progressive revelation in Scripture and in relationship with us.

You may wonder why this has to be so complex. Why can't
He just be "God" and let that be all we need to know? In his
book *The Deep Things of God*, Fred Sanders said,

> God's way of being God is to be Father, Son,
> and Holy Spirit simultaneously from all eter-
> nity, perfectly complete in a triune fellowship
> of love. If we don't take this as our starting
> point, everything we say about the practical
> relevance of the Trinity could lead us to one
> colossal misunderstanding: thinking of God
> the Trinity as a means to some other end.[8]

If we preferred worshipping the version of Him we've
imagined instead of getting to know who He really is, we'd
be guilty of idolatry at worst and laziness at best. And on top
of that, we'd be missing out on some of the most beautiful
aspects of who He is and the joy that comes from knowing
Him more!

There are things we can't see about Him if we don't look closely at His tri-unity. For instance, if God were uni-personal instead of triune, He couldn't be love in His essence. It would be something He does, not something He is because He wouldn't have been capable of love until He created something to love. Love requires an "other." That means He would've been Creator before He was Love, and His love would be attached to His accomplishments. But since He has always been a community of love within Himself, then love is at the core of who He is. He has always been other oriented. God faces outward. Tim Keller said this means that "love is cosmic ultimate reality." Keller goes on to explain that without the Trinity, the ultimate reality of love falls apart.[9] For instance, polytheists worship gods who are contending for power, not love. In eastern religions, where god is merely a force, their god is impersonal and can't contain love, be love, or give love.

One of the ways we see the love within the Godhead (another name for the Trinity) is when they talk to or about each other. This happens most often in the New Testament. In the Gospels, we get to eavesdrop on Jesus's prayer life where He talks directly to the Father, and we also hear Him describing the work of the Holy Spirit to His disciples. These conversations reveal not only that Father, Son, and Holy Spirit are three distinct Persons but that they're each focused on the others, deferring to them and pointing toward their glory out of their love for each other. It becomes clear that they aim to **glorify** each other.

As you explore God's diversity of Persons as seen in Scripture, a helpful exercise is to consider who is speaking, who the speaker is speaking *to*, and what the speaker is speaking *about*. The verses below provide an example as you explore the Bible and find God's triune nature within it:

> And a voice from heaven said, "This is my beloved Son, with whom I am well-pleased." (Matt. 3:17 CSB)

> **Q:** Who is speaking?
> **A:** God the Father

> **Q:** Who is He speaking to?
> **A:** God the Son, Jesus, at His baptism, along with the crowd gathered at Jesus's baptism

> **Q:** What is He speaking about?
> **A:** His pleasure in His Son

> While he was still speaking, suddenly a bright cloud covered them, and a voice from the cloud said, "This is my beloved Son, with whom I am well-pleased. Listen to him!" (Matt. 17:5 CSB)

> **Q:** Who is speaking?
> **A:** God the Father

> **Q:** Who is He speaking to?
> **A:** Those gathered at Jesus's transfiguration

Q: What is He speaking about?

A: His pleasure in His Son and a command to others to listen to His Son.

"Father, if you are willing, take this cup away from me—nevertheless, not my will, but yours, be done." (Luke 22:42 csb)

> **Q:** Who is speaking?
> **A:** Jesus, God the Son, in the garden of Gethsemane right before His crucifixion

> **Q:** Who is He speaking to?
> **A:** God the Father

> **Q:** What is He speaking about?
> **A:** The wrath He is about to endure on the cross and His trust in God the Father's plan

"But the Counselor, the Holy Spirit, whom the Father will send in my name, will teach you all things and remind you of everything I have told you." (John 14:26 csb)

> **Q:** Who is speaking?
> **A:** Jesus, God the Son

> **Q:** Who is He speaking to?
> **A:** His followers

Q: What is He speaking about?
A: The Holy Spirit's ministry to
believers

"So that the world may know that I love the
Father, I do as the Father commanded me."
(John 14:31 csb)

> **Q:** Who is speaking?
> **A:** Jesus, God the Son
>
> **Q:** Who is He speaking to?
> **A:** His followers
>
> **Q:** What is He speaking about?
> **A:** His relationship with God the
> Father; His obedience to God the
> Father

"Nevertheless, I am telling you the truth. It
is for your benefit that I go away, because if
I don't go away the Counselor will not come
to you. If I go, I will send him to you." (John
16:7 csb)

> **Q:** Who is speaking?
> **A:** Jesus, God the Son
>
> **Q:** Who is He speaking to?
> **A:** His followers
>
> **Q:** What is He speaking about?

A: The goodness and the ministry of the Holy Spirit

"Father, I want those you have given me to be with me where I am, so that they will see my glory, which you have given me because you loved me before the world's foundation." (John 17:24 csb)

Q: Who is speaking?
A: Jesus, God the Son

Q: Who is He speaking to?
A: God the Father, in prayer

Q: What is He speaking about?
A: A prayer for spiritual sight and unity among His disciples and for His followers to see the loving relationship between God the Father and God the Son

It's amazing to see just how much the Father, Son, and Spirit show up together in the Scriptures, isn't it?

In our journey to know God better (and experience more joy!), we've now covered the fact that God is a *revealer*. We've also covered His *unity* and His *diversity*. The final aspect about God we will explore in this chapter so that we may know Him better is His trinitarian *relationships*.

God's Relationships

In the previous section, we saw how much the Trinity loves each other, points to each other, and glorifies each other. Their actions are motivated by love! And because this is all built on and fueled by perfect love, that means there is deep, abiding, gospel joy at the heart of the Trinity. That joy is not just contained within God Himself—it's joy for us too!

God is inherently relational. In this section, we'll look at two general categories of God's relationships: His relationship within the Trinity and His relationship with humanity.

What we've been talking about up to this point is primarily God's relationship within Himself—the Father, the Son, and the Spirit. This internal life of God is what theologians often refer to as the **Immanent Trinity** because *immanent* means "existing or operating within; inherent."[10] (Note: Some theologians prefer to use the term *Ontological Trinity* instead of *Immanent Trinity*. Both titles refer to the same thing.)

This term points to all the things we've covered in the previous sections about how God operates within Himself, the inner life of the divine community of the Father, Son, and Spirit. "God is love" within Himself. Even though we all love hearing about ourselves, it's important that we cover this relationship first because, as Fred Sanders said, "God is Trinity primarily for himself and only secondarily for us."[11] If that comes as a shock or a surprise, hang in there—we'll eventually see why this is not only important but also comforting. It would be wrong to think of ourselves as God's primary focal point and purpose; that is not the message of Scripture.

The closer we lean in to see Him, the more we'll discover about Him and the more His joy will embed itself into our lives. He created us and invited us into a preexisting joy. Scripture never tells us why God created the world and mankind, but it does tell us what God was doing before He made us. For all eternity, He has been and is and will be reveling in infinite communal love, which means God is infinitely happy! If God were singular, His reasons for creating the world would've been rooted in need, boredom, loneliness, or power—all of which would point to His selfishness in creating. Instead, He was already fulfilled in His triune perfection.

Consider John 17:24:

> "Father, I want those you have given me to
> be with me where I am, so that they will see
> my glory, which you have given me because
> **you loved me before the world's foundation**."
> (csb, emphasis added)

What was God doing before He created the world? Love. And this wasn't a one-way love; the persons of God point outside themselves to each other as a result of love.

Consider also the following verses (and their context) and notice who was glorifying/pointing to whom:

> "When the Spirit of truth comes, he will guide
> you into all the truth. For he will not speak on

his own, but he will speak whatever he hears.
He will also declare to you what is to come. He
will glorify me, because he will take from what
is mine and declare it to you. Everything the
Father has is mine. This is why I told you that
he takes from what is mine and will declare it
to you." (John 16:13–15 csb)

> The Spirit will glorify Jesus.
> The Spirit will declare the words of
>   Jesus.
> The words of Jesus are from the Father.

"I have glorified you on the earth by complet-
ing the work you gave me to do. Now, Father,
glorify me in your presence with that glory I
had with you before the world existed." (John
17:4–5 csb)

> Jesus glorified the Father.
> Jesus asked the Father to glorify Him.

Do you see how the focal point of each Person of the
Trinity is on another Person of the Trinity? If humans were
God's focal point, He would be unfulfilled without us, which
means He wouldn't be infinitely happy. We want and need a
happy God, so it's good news for us that He is! Fred Sanders
said, "The boundless life that God lives in himself, at home,
within the happy land of the Trinity above all worlds, is perfect.

It is complete, inexhaustibly full, and infinitely blessed."[12] If we look at Acts 17:24–25 (csb), we see this emphasized in Scripture's teachings of the early church as well:

> The God who made the world and everything in it—he is Lord of heaven and earth—does not live in shrines made by hands. Neither is he served by human hands, as though he needed anything, since he himself gives everyone life and breath and all things.

Notice the dual truths the Bible keeps holding out in front of us: (1) God needs nothing from humans because He is already happy in Himself, and out of the overflow of that happiness and love, He created humanity. And (2) humans need everything from God!

Again, God needs nothing. That's why He can love so well. This is the best hint we have about why God would create the world—out of an overflow of His infinite love and happiness!

This brings us to the second category of God's relationships; it's something theologians often refer to as the **Economic Trinity**. The word *economic* comes from the Greek word *oikonomia*, which means *household management*.[13] This phrase essentially relates to how the triune God works outside of Himself and, more specifically, within His family. (That's us!) It refers to all the ways God's personal love spills out into the world.

Before we move deeper into this, let's summarize the internal/external relationships of the Trinity.

Immanent Trinity (internal relationships that pertain to being)

- The Father is the Father because He eternally begets the Son.
- The Son is the Son because He is eternally begotten of the Father.
- The Spirit is the Spirit because He eternally proceeds from the Father, through the Son.

Economic Trinity (external relationships that pertain to doing)

- The Father sent the Son.
- The Son is sent by/of the Father.
- The Spirit is sent by/of the Father and the Son.

These details undergird everything else we'll cover in this study. We will spend time focusing on specific ways the **Economic Trinity** engages with humanity, but it's important to remember that everything God does flows from who He is, not the other way around. "Trinity" is not the work uniform He puts on when He deals with humanity; it's who He has always been throughout all eternity, unchanged.

You're probably already familiar with some of the major aspects of God's external work—it includes creation, salvation, and restoration. We tend to assign certain works to certain persons of the Trinity—we may think of the Father as the One who created the world, the Son as the One who saved us, etc.—but Scripture reveals that each Person of the Trinity is active in the whole process. While they each have unique roles, they have one shared goal and are each vital in God's relationship with His children.

First Peter 1:1–2 shows us a good example of this. While it may be common to consider Jesus as the sole person who saves us by His sacrifice on the cross, look at how Peter explains the work of salvation:

> Peter, an apostle of Jesus Christ: To those chosen, living as exiles dispersed abroad in Pontus, Galatia, Cappadocia, Asia, and Bithynia, **chosen according to the foreknowledge of God the Father,** through the **sanctifying work of the Spirit,** to be obedient and to be sprinkled with the **blood of Jesus Christ**. May grace and peace be multiplied to you. (csb, emphasis added)

Notice how this isn't just a "Jesus" thing—each person of the Trinity has a role and a common goal in the process of adopting people into God's family. Your salvation, my friend, is a gift from not just Christ but the triune God!

Fred Sanders frequently reiterates in his writings, "The Trinity is the gospel."[14] Without the active engagement of any one of them in our lives, our rescue would fall apart. Inasmuch as they all point to each other and seek to glorify each other in their unity, they work together to pour that love out toward us. The cross demonstrates the infinite loving heart of God to us. It shows us who God has been all along, independent of us. This is why it's so important that God's triune nature is first for Him and secondarily for us. Since we have a God who is already completely fulfilled within Himself, He delights to share that unity and joy! "If this is true," Tim Keller said, "then your absolute highest purpose, your meaning, and the only way you'll ever be happy is if you are glorifying God above all other things."[15] As we seek to live for God's glory, we'll get the joy and delight that comes as a result.

Love is inherent to who God is. That's what He has extended to us and invited us into. He wants joy for you, and that's why He draws you near—because He's where the joy is!

2

God the Father

Three Foundations of the Trinity

1. There is only one true God.
2. There are three divine Persons of the one true God.
3. The three Persons are co-equal,
co-eternal, and co-relational.

Why Father?

As we begin to look closer at God the Father, I want to acknowledge that some of you may bristle at that name/title and for good reason—you've had *or lacked* someone in your life who should've demonstrated what a good father looked like, and they failed you miserably. They wounded you in ways that make God your heavenly Father angry and that break His heart.

Some of the best men and women I know had terrible fathers. Maybe yours was terrible too or even altogether absent. If that's your story, you may have a hard time warming up to God the Father and want to keep Him at a distance. Even if your earthly father was good, his imperfections might skew your view of the heavenly Father. If you struggle to connect with God the Father and prefer to focus on Jesus or the Spirit, I'm asking God to begin to redeem the word *father* for you, starting now—to meet you in this chapter and speak the truth to your heart.

So, why would God choose the word *Father* for Himself? There were certainly other options. Why didn't He opt for a term that doesn't carry so much baggage? Wouldn't we all prefer "God the Grandmother Who Gives Us Unlimited Ice Cream"? I'm inclined to think God had a redemption story up His sleeve here—as He always does when it comes to His kids. Not only was He the good Father before all our other fathers got it wrong, but He's the One who enters into all the voids they've left behind. The name "father" belongs to Him before it belonged to anyone who may have sinned against you, and He knows how to love you perfectly.

Because He's our only chance to see what a father should be, I don't want us to miss it! I believe He has good things in store for you on these particular pages.

In chapter 1, we learned that the persons of the Trinity are **consubstantial**—they have the same essence, and each fully possesses/is the divine essence. So when we see the character of Jesus or the Spirit revealed to us, we also see what the Father is like. If you're drawn to Jesus or the Spirit but you struggle with the Father, let this set your heart at ease: they are revealing Him to you. What you find lovely about each of them is also in Him. Because Jesus and the Spirit have the same attributes as the Father, that means anything you find beautiful about them exists in Him too.

In a patrilineal society—cultures where the father's line is what connects each subsequent generation—the one who gives identity to another person is known as a "father." Both fathers and mothers contribute to the identities of their offspring, but God has specifically chosen to identify Himself as Father, not Mother—though not because He is male. (Since He doesn't have a physical body, He can't be male in the sense that we think of it.) But in this patrilineal society, "Father" gives us the best understanding of the role He plays not only toward us but toward the other persons of the Trinity as well. The Father is Father because He eternally begets and loves the Son.

We honor others by referring to them with the name they use to introduce themselves. For all of us who have been adopted into His family, God says He is our Father. **Even though He's the Creator of every single human, He's only the Father to those who yield their lives to Jesus** (see John

1:11–12; 1 John 3:1; 5:1–2). We have the right and the privilege of knowing Him in this kind of intimate, relational way. We honor Him when we call Him Father.

Just as you want to be called by your name, we honor God by thinking of Him as Father and calling Him Father; it's consistent with what He has told us about who He is, and He cannot lie. Addressing God this way doesn't just honor Him; it's a huge honor to us too! The fact that the God of the universe invites sinful humans to refer to Him as "Father" is remarkable! He delights to be in a relationship with us. He doesn't turn His nose up at us or roll His eyes; He calls us His beloved children. In his book *Delighting in the Trinity*, Michael Reeves puts it this way:

> For if God is not a Father, if he has no Son and will have no children, then he must be lonely, distant and unapproachable; if he is not triune and so not essentially loving, then no God at all just looks better.[1]

Without Him fathering within the Trinity first, there would be no us. Without a relational triune God, there would be no overflow of love, no catalyst for creation. His being corresponds to His doing. Because in eternity past, the Father, Son, and Spirit have always been who they will always eternally be, their roles for their relationship with humanity follow their identities. For the Father, those roles include being the initiator, the architect of creation. We recognize Jesus's death on the cross as the greatest act of love the world has ever known—and it is—but that monumental event that serves as the foundation of our faith was part of the Father's plan. There's nothing the Son or the Spirit did or does that isn't somehow anchored in the Father's planning and initiation. They do nothing apart from Him. But don't take my word for it; consider how Jesus Himself puts it when He speaks of His dependence on and alignment with the Father's will and plan:

> "The Son can do nothing of his own accord, but only what he sees the Father doing. For whatever the Father does, that the Son does likewise." (John 5:19)

> "I have come down from heaven, not to do my own will, but the will of him who sent me." (John 6:38 csb)

> [Jesus] fell facedown and prayed, "My Father, if it is possible, let this cup pass from me. Yet not as I will, but as you will." (Matt. 26:39 csb)

> "My food is to do the will of him who sent me and to finish his work," Jesus told them. (John 4:34 csb)

> "I can do nothing on my own. I judge only as I hear, and my judgment is just, because I do

not seek my own will, but the will of him who
sent me." (John 5:30 csʙ)

So Jesus said to them, "When you lift up the
Son of Man, then you will know that I am he,
and that I do nothing on my own. But just
as the Father taught me, I say these things."
(John 8:28 csʙ)

The Father's good plan and generous will are connected to
every good thing we experience with the Son and the Spirit.
He's far more winsome and compassionate than the reputation
we sometimes give Him via misinformation we've received or
our own misperception. In order to help us understand the
Father better and gain perspective on His words and actions,
we'll spend the rest of this chapter looking at who He is, what
He's like, and what He does. This order is important because
actions are born out of who someone is and what that person
is like, but as we look at each section in detail, we'll see lots
of overlap since "being" and "doing" are so interwoven. We'll
start by looking at the first relationships He ever had, the first
relationships to ever exist: the Father within the Trinity.

The Father in Relationship

God's good plan started long before He created us. Think
about this: He was Father before He was Creator. He didn't
become the Father. He's *always been* fathering within the Trinity.

And out of the overflow of love within the Trinity, He created us. You exist out of love, created by love, to be so moved by His love for you that you love Him in return (1 John 4:19). That's why you're here on earth. You weren't an accident or an oversight but a carefully planned, lovingly designed image bearer of God who is now also a child of God, intentionally adopted into His family—for His glory and delight and for your freedom and joy.

He didn't need to do this. **He didn't need us. He wanted to create us out of His divine overflow of love.** Nothing in Scripture indicates that He was lonely or bored before we showed up on the scene. Instead, when Scripture points to what reality was like before time itself was created, it points to each Person of the Trinity being occupied with love for the other Persons of the Trinity. Even without creation or redemption, God would still be who He is, which is who He has always been—triune, self-existent, and full of love.

Creation is where we first see the roles of the Trinity emerging. But before God took any direct action toward creating humanity, He existed in all of His perfection and glory. Before He was a Creator, He was a Father—not the Father of us (not yet, anyway) but the Father within the Trinity itself. He needed nothing, and the fullness of His triune nature— Father, Son, and Spirit—dwelled together in perfect love. Out of the overflow of their love, God the Father set His plan in motion to create us and establish a relationship with us.

Creating is the first way we see Him taking action in Scripture, but that's because this is where we enter the story. Of course, God's story began long before ours did. He was fully God before He made anything. It's important to note that His God-ness isn't contingent upon His being the Creator; otherwise, He wouldn't have been God until the moment He created. His position as Deity would have relied on causing us to exist. In that sense, He would need us in order to be who He is. But He is dependent on nothing, and everything is dependent on Him. Even before time began, the Father has always been the Father.

In John 17:24, when Jesus was speaking to the Father, He said, "You loved me before the foundation of the world." Before there was ever a creation or a command, there was a Father and His love. He has always loved the Son and the Spirit. The fact that the Father has been loving perfectly for all eternity tells us a lot about who He is. Whenever Scripture peels back the curtain on eternity, we see a glimpse of His great love and His plan to demonstrate that love.

When people first consider God, they may think of Him as merely "Creator" in the Old Testament, ruling and reigning over all the peoples of the earth in whatever way He sees fit, and then switch to considering Him as "loving Father" in the New Testament once Jesus comes on the scene and speaks often about God the Father. But when we hold such a fractionated view of the Father, it's impossible to have an accurate understanding of how His words and actions connect us to

His heart. Gaining a fuller understanding of who He reveals Himself to be throughout the *whole* of Scripture is the only way we'll ever grasp the magnitude of His love for us!

God knew we needed to see our need for Him, and He had a brilliant, generous plan to help us realize it, not just at the start of the New Testament but all the way back at the beginning of the Old! Like any parent with a willful, rebellious kid, He let Adam and Eve experience the natural consequences of their own defiance. As a result of the sin they brought into the world in the first few chapters of Genesis, God's good creation devolves into murder, slavery, and oppression, clearly needing some sort of rescue plan.

It's not just the sin of Adam and Eve that needed redemption; *our* sin makes it obvious that we need a rescue plan, too—one that can only come from outside ourselves. And the good news for us is this: *God planned that rescue before the fall of man ever happened.* Just listen to how Paul explains it in the book of Ephesians:

> Blessed is the God and Father of our Lord Jesus Christ, who has blessed us with every spiritual blessing in the heavens in Christ. For **he chose us** in him, **before the foundation of the world,** to be holy and blameless in love before him. He predestined us **to be adopted as sons through Jesus Christ for himself, according to the good pleasure of his will,**

to the praise of his glorious grace that he lavished on us in the Beloved One.

In him we have redemption through his blood, the forgiveness of our trespasses, according to the riches of his grace that he richly poured out on us with all wisdom and understanding. He made known to us the mystery of his will, according to his good pleasure that he purposed in Christ **as a plan for the right time**—to bring everything together in Christ, both things in heaven and things on earth in him.

In him we have also received an inheritance, because we were predestined **according to the plan** of the one who works out everything in agreement with the purpose of his will, so that we who had already put our hope in Christ might bring praise to his glory. (Eph. 1:3–12 csb, emphasis added)

In Bible passages like Matthew 25:34 and Revelation 13:8, we get glimpses of what it looks like for the triune God to exist outside of time, and they reveal that His love and His plan preceded not just our existence but the world's existence. According to these verses, the names of His children were written in the Book of Life, and a kingdom was prepared for them to enjoy "before the foundation of the world."

The Father was loving perfectly within the Trinity and making plans and provision for His children before the earth was founded. This gives us a glimpse into His character and His heart toward His kids. Before we even fell, God had a plan to redeem us from the fall. Sending His Son Jesus to pay our sin debt wasn't plan B. Jesus was always plan A. God has no plan B. **Rescue and redemption have always been the Father's plan.**

As we can see now, if we only see God as Creator and not as Father, we miss out on the relational aspect that God called us to and created us for. We become a product, and He becomes nothing more than our distant, uncaring producer who has moved on to other projects.

But on the other hand, if we see God as *only* Father, without seeing Him through the lens of the fullness of the triune God, there's a good chance we'll become legalists, especially if we attach our understanding of Him to the experiences we've had with our earthly fathers. We may try to do all the right things to please the Father out of fear of punishment. We have to rightly understand who we're in this relationship with by seeing Him as He exists within the Trinity. To do that, we have to start before the beginning. In other words, we cannot get ourselves right until we get Him right. And we cannot get Him right until we get Them right.

Our origin story starts not only with God the Father but with the eternal triune God, existing in perfect love and unity before the foundation of the world. God created us out of relationship, for relationship. "Then God said, 'Let us make man in our image, after our likeness.' . . . So God created man in his own image, in the image of God he created him; male and female he created them" (Gen. 1:26–27). You exist to be loved by God and to be so moved by His love for you that you love Him in return (1 John 4:19).

We must make an important clarification when we refer to God as our Father. According to Scripture, the only way people can approach the Father as their own Father is through the finished work of God the Son and the presence of the Spirit. They always work in unison because, as the second foundation of the Trinity reminds us, there can be no separation. As we've noted before, our salvation and adoption into God's family is the work of all three Persons of the Trinity. Consider how each Person of the Trinity is at work in these verses:

- In John 14:6, Jesus said, "I am the way, and the truth, and the life. No one comes to the Father except through me."

  Here we see Jesus on full display when it comes to being adopted by the Father.

- In Romans 15:16–17, Paul says he is a "minister of Christ Jesus to the Gentiles in the priestly service" of what? "The gospel of God."

Why? "So that the offering of the Gentiles may be acceptable, sanctified by the Holy Spirit."

What's the result? "In Christ Jesus, then, I have reason to be proud of my work for God."

Here we see the gospel was something not merely related to Christ Jesus but "of God" the Father *and* something requiring the Spirit's sanctification. All three Persons of the Trinity are on full display when it comes to gospel work.

- In Titus 3:3–7, Paul says, "For we ourselves were once foolish, disobedient, led astray, slaves to various passions and pleasures, passing our days in malice and envy, hated by others and hating one another. But when the goodness and loving kindness of God our Savior appeared, he saved us, not because of works done by us in righteousness, but according to his own mercy, by the washing of regeneration and renewal of the Holy Spirit, whom he poured out on us richly through Jesus Christ our Savior, so that being justified by his grace we might become heirs according to the hope of eternal life."

Here we see the love of God appearing
in the Person of the Savior, Christ, who
saved us not just by His own blood but
also by the regenerative work of the Holy
Spirit. (And notice how we can't experience the Spirit's work alone on an island.
His renewing work can only be poured out
on us by the Father through Jesus Christ.)
Again, all three Persons of the Trinity are
on full display when it comes to how our
salvation and adoption into the Father's
family gets accomplished!

This is an important distinction: while God is the Creator
of all creation, He is not the Father of all creation. All humans
are His image bearers and His creation, but the only way we
become His children is by adoption into His family. In His
great kindness, He adopts some of humanity into His family
to be coheirs with His Son Jesus. If we misunderstand how we
become God's children, we risk losing sight of the gospel. We
only have God as our Father when we repent, place our faith
in His Son Christ, and are changed by his indwelling Spirit.
This occurs when we see the need for His work in our lives.
We must recognize our desperation. Jesus referred to this as
being "poor in spirit," and He called it a blessing (Matt. 5:3).
In modern terms, we might call this *spiritual poverty*; it's the
awareness that we have nothing to offer God, which leads us

to Jesus. When we acknowledge Jesus as Savior and Lord and receive the Holy Spirit, we're made part of God's family!

Here are a few of the times Scripture points to this distinction of God being the Father only of believers:

In John 8:42–44, Jesus said this:

> "If God were your Father, you would love me, for I came from God and I am here. I came not of my own accord, but he sent me. Why do you not understand what I say? It is because you cannot bear to hear my word. You are of your father the devil."

From this verse, we can see that God cannot be called Father of those who do not love His Son. Rather, for those who reject Christ, Jesus says they are of a different father, "the devil."

When Jesus paid our sin debt, He not only took on our sins, but He granted us His righteousness. And when we receive Christ, we receive His perfect righteousness, which makes us fit for God's family. John 1:12 says it this way:

> To all who did receive him, who believed in his name, he gave the right to become children of God.

As a sign of our adoption and a "seal" of His approval, the Father sends His Spirit to live in us (Eph. 1:13). When that happens, our relationship with the Father is fixed forever, and we bear His name, just as an adopted child takes on the adoptive family name. Paul said it this way in Romans 8:9–11:

> Anyone who does not have the Spirit of
> Christ does not belong to him. But if Christ
> is in you, although the body is dead because of
> sin, the Spirit is life because of righteousness.
> If the Spirit of him who raised Jesus from the
> dead dwells in you, he who raised Christ Jesus
> from the dead will also give life to your mortal
> bodies through his Spirit who dwells in you.

Because of the finished work of Christ on the cross, God's Spirit comes to dwell within His kids as markers of this new identity. So take heart: God didn't just want to save you and move on; He wanted to live *with* you and *in* you! As God's child, here's what you need to know: everything driving His relationship with you is fueled by trinitarian love. All of God's words and work are intended for your joy and flourishing. Does He hate your sin? Absolutely. But if you are in Christ, then as your Father, all His wrath for your sin was poured out on Jesus on the cross. There is none left for you now that you are His child.

It may be easy for some to focus only on the fact that God punishes sin—and that is an important aspect of who He is—but His punishment of sin is fueled not by cruelty but by love. We all naturally hate anything that threatens the thing we love. God hates sin; sin robs you and distorts you! God, however, is after both His glory and your flourishing. You've been adopted into His eternal family, lavished with righteousness and love, and He works in all of that to help you look more like Him, to display Him to the world. God wants His kids to look like Him!

As we wrap up this section, I don't know if I can say it any better than J. I. Packer in his book *Knowing God*:

> If you want to judge how well a person understands Christianity, find out how much he makes of the thought of being God's child, and having God as his Father. If this is not the thought that prompts and controls his worship and prayers and his whole outlook on life, it means that he does not understand Christianity very well at all.[2]

The Father's Character (How He Is)

When evangelicals lose their sense of proportion, they begin to talk as if they no longer care about the character of God unless they get something from it. The best defense against this has always been the doctrine of the eternal Trinity in itself.
—Fred Sanders[3]

Performing religious actions without having an affection for God is similar to a loveless marriage. If God's interaction

with us was just Him ruling over us, He would only want
obedience. But because He is a personal, relational God, He
wants to love and be loved. Jonathan Edwards said, "True religion, in a great measure, consists in holy affections."[4] We've
been invited into the most beautiful relationship a human
could ever know, but we will miss the sheer delight of it all if
we view Him wrongly.

God spends the whole story of Scripture revealing Himself
to us. Scripture is not primarily our to-do list; it is our "to
behold" list. We come to Scripture to look for God—what He
loves, what He hates, who He is, what motivates Him to do
what He does. When we pay attention to what's revealed, we
see He's a God who loves and whose wrath and justice abide
perfectly with that love. These characteristics aren't in conflict
with each other; they work in unison. How so? We all hate
anything that threatens the things we love. We want to protect
what we love. And that's how God works too. He wants to
protect us from harm because He loves us.

We've already established that God is love within Himself,
the Trinity, so we know God loves God. That is right and good
because He is nothing less than perfectly lovely. Scripture tells
us God also loves us, His children. First John 3:1 says, "See
what kind of love the Father has given to us, that we should be
called children of God; and so we are." Since God loves God
and God loves His kids, He laid out some fatherly, protective
rules for us.

God first began making His laws known in the garden of Eden. Adam and Eve had only one law (Gen. 2:17), and the enemy used that one law to prompt them to wonder if God really had their best interests at heart. They doubted Him based on one law. From the start, we see humanity didn't understand who God is; they perceived Him to be cruel. When they sinned, they hid from Him. They didn't believe His love, so they were driven by fear. After all, God had said that on the day they broke His law, they would die.

But, shockingly, when God pursued them, He didn't kill them. He clothed them. Even their sin revealed His love for them. But in some ways, the day they sinned, they did die—they lost the kind of life God intended for humanity. Their eventual physical deaths were symptomatic of the curse of being cut off from God's special presence. Romans 5:12 makes clear that Adam's sin brought about death—physical and eternal—for all of us. But God's response to their sin, and ours, was redemption. He exemplified it (Gen. 3:21) and pointed toward it (Gen. 3:15).

As we move further into the Old Testament, we encounter the Israelites, God's people. They'd been enslaved for four hundred years. By the time God set them free, they had no reason to trust authority. They'd never lived in a free society and had no idea how to keep order. God gave them instructions—commandments—for building a healthy society. He established laws to help them honor Him and others so they could flourish. But they couldn't keep the laws. Did God smite them or give up on them? No. He set up camp—literally—in the middle of a bunch of sinners to live with them!

Forty years after God moved them from slavery in Egypt to freedom in the wilderness, He moved them again—into the promised land. With all the new opportunities at hand, He gave them more information on how to live in their new land (Deut. 7:1–5), how important it was for them to obey His commands (Deut. 11), and how to honor their new kings and each other (Deut. 17:14–20). But still they resisted. All along, God told them their failure to keep His laws would lead to the downfall of their society. And despite God's mercy and great patience, that's what happened. Their continued disobedience led to devastation and exile.

When it comes to understanding God, here's our problem: if we drop down in the middle of this story, it can seem like "Old Testament God" is harsh and demanding. We wonder which laws apply to us and which we can sidestep without angering Him. If that's the case, we've lost the plot. This is a love story—a story about flourishing and joy! We have to zoom out to remember that this story was set in motion by our great initiating God who was motivated by the overflow of His love. And He wants to be loved back (Matt. 22:36–40). He has a plan to build a relationship with people. That alone is shocking because He's perfect ("complete") and holy ("set apart"), and we are not. We are broken people who never miss an opportunity to do the wrong thing. Yet He leans in; He doesn't run from us or turn His back.

Do you know how I know we've lost the plot? The Israelites, sinful as they were, showed a pattern of rejoicing when God gave them commands. Psalm 119 is the longest chapter in the Bible, and the whole thing is a tribute to God's laws and His kindness in giving them His laws. Why are our responses so different from the original audience?

In Egypt, and in their new land, the Israelites were surrounded by a bunch of pagans who worshipped a variety of gods—some of which they made by hand and others they attached to things like the sun or the weather. This meant the pagans had no idea how to please their gods. They were left guessing. They tried sacrificing their children, cutting themselves, having sex with animals—you name it. They had no instruction manual, no true prophets to guide them.

So when God showed up and reintroduced Himself to His people, His requirements were a great act of kindness to them. What a relief! He told them how and why things worked the way they did in their relationship with Him. He also said they were going to get it all terribly wrong but that in His kindness He had already made a way to set things right. From the beginning, He dropped breadcrumbs throughout the Old Testament, pointing to Jesus. In fact, Jesus confirmed that the Old Testament testified about Him (Luke 24:25–27; John 5:39–40).

It's easiest to see the multifaceted love of God when we have a view of the whole story. That's how we prefer to experience most stories—none of us drop down in the middle of a movie, stay for five minutes, and expect to understand the plot. We need context.

Without the broader context of the whole of Scripture, it's easy to view God wrongly. Some people prefer to focus on His love and don't think about how much He hates sin. Others feel condemnation and shame when they sin and have a hard time feeling His love for them. But we have to see the full scope of who God has revealed Himself to be—not just pieces of Him—or our lives will be built on half-truths that lead us further from intimacy with Him.

Here are a few of the ways that might play out:

A. If we see only God's justice or wrath but not His love, we'll distance ourselves from Him out of fear. And if we dare to try to draw near to Him, we'll only do it to avoid punishment or earn favor instead of simply drawing near because we love Him. Or we may attempt to clean ourselves up so we can be acceptable to Him—hoping our good deeds outweigh our bad ones so we can "make the cut." And because all our efforts to earn God's favor will leave us fearful and striving, we'll miss out on the joy of intimacy with Him.

B. If we see only God's love but not His justice or wrath, we'll turn Him into a two-dimensional character. He'll be the "yes-man" who does our bidding. We'll become spoiled and entitled. We'll grow angry when He doesn't bow to our whims and give us exactly what we want exactly when we want it. We'll be frustrated with Him any time He answers our prayers with a no. And again, we'll miss out on the joy of intimacy with Him.

C. If we don't believe in God at all—His love or His wrath—we'll become our own gods. We'll spend our lives in self-improvement or selfish pursuits. They may bring us temporary happiness, but we will always feel vulnerable because when the things we love most are earthly things, they can always be taken away. When we're in the midst of trials, we won't have the certainty of a peace-drenched eternity that sets the deepest places of our souls at rest. You guessed it—we'll miss the joy of intimacy with Him.

God wants intimacy with You. He delights in you. "The LORD takes pleasure in his people" (Ps. 149:4). Pleasure! That means He doesn't just love you. He likes you. He wants to hang out with you. Not just for a few hours on Sunday when you clean yourself up and put your best foot forward but always. That's why He came to dwell *in* you and promises to never leave. Zephaniah 3:17 says, "The LORD your God is among you, a warrior who saves. He will rejoice over you with gladness. He will be quiet in his love. *He will delight in you with singing*" (CSB, emphasis added).

Notice that both of the verses we just read (Ps. 149:4 and Zeph. 3:17) are in the Old Testament—the very place where people often reduce God to wrath. Instead, He's demonstrating His great love for you even there. That's because He is always the same—yesterday, today, forever. He has been working out His plan for redemption all along. Jesus was the fulfillment of that plan. Can you see it now? **The Father didn't get *kinder* when Jesus came to earth. He was always kind.**

Here's an analogy: if you're a parent, imagine you've bought a present for your daughter for her birthday. You hide it away for a few months, then give it to her when the day comes. What if she *only* thought you were kind on the day you gave her the gift? What if she thought you were cruel and withholding on all the days prior? Wouldn't you feel misunderstood? You know without a shadow of a doubt that you've loved her all along, even on the days when she was waiting for the gift or didn't even know it existed.

Redemption has always been the gift the Father had planned for us. He set His plan in motion before He created the earth; then, at the right time, Jesus was the revealing and fulfilling of that plan, His work applied to us through the power of the Spirit. And even after receiving such a gift, we await another gift: the day Christ comes back to restore all the things we've broken. When we take all these things together, we realize God wasn't just good at the resurrection. Nor will He be good only on the day when Jesus returns. He has always been and will always be equally good—yesterday, today, forever.

Only in seeing God rightly—in His great goodness and love and holiness—can we learn to see ourselves rightly. As we look at Him, we'll inevitably see that we fall short of His standards. All our sin accrues a debt we could never pay. Every doubt, every mixed motive, every selfish thought and word—all earn us punishment and separation from God. It's what we deserve (Rom. 3:10–20, 23). But the love-soaked plan of the Father, the sacrifice of Jesus, and the renewing and sanctifying work of the Spirit have made a way for us. When we turn from our sin and turn to Him in faith, we find forgiveness.

One of the most beautiful paradoxes in Scripture is where God's utter holiness (set-apart-ness) meets His relentless pursuit of sinners. It's shocking to read the whole story and see that He never stopped wanting to be near those sinners, including you and me! He has united Himself to us inextricably through Christ, and this union is our greatest freedom and our deepest joy!

The Father's Actions (What He Does)

Since God is, before all things, a Father, and not primarily Creator or Ruler, all his ways are beautifully fatherly. It is not that this God "does" being Father as a day job, only to kick back in the evenings as plain old "God." It is not that he has a nice blob of fatherly icing on top. He is Father. All the way down. Thus all that he does he does as Father. —Michael Reeves[5]

In this section, we'll look specifically at the work God the Father has done in the story of our redemption. One of the challenging parts about these chapters on the individual Persons of the Trinity is that it's impossible to divide the work of God up from Person to Person. They're all collectively engaged in each aspect of their work with humanity. However, they each serve different roles in that work.

As the authority (which comes from the same root as "author") in the **Economic Trinity**, the Father is the initiator of all good things we experience (James 1:17). He initiated the universe. He initiated mankind. He initiated a relationship with us. He is the One who set all these things in motion. He delights to pursue us out of love, and we'll find our deepest joy in trusting and responding to His love as it reaches out to us through all His actions!

He's a real person with a real personality, and His personality consists not only of love but of wrath and justice and myriad other things. We can't remake Him to be what we want Him to be. So if this is who He is, then we may be tempted to avoid Him on the bad days when He's leaning into wrath, right? We'll continue to dig into this, but as a first step, I want to point out some beautiful hints Scripture gives us about God's personality and character, which are inextricably linked to who He is and what He does. He is far more than a one-dimensional being, and some of the ways He interacts are unique to those who are His children. All God does in relation to His children is done as Father. For example:

- He created (Gen. 1:1–3).
- He disciplines (Deut. 8:5).

- He delivers (Ps. 18:2).
- He shows compassion (Ps. 103:13).
- He provides (Matt. 6:28–30).
- He delights to give (Luke 12:32).
- He draws us in (John 6:44).
- He keeps us (John 10:29).
- He pours out love and His Spirit to us (Rom. 5:5).
- He gave us His Son (Rom. 8:32).
- He is both kind and severe (Rom. 11:22).
- He initiated our adoption (Gal. 4:4–5; Eph. 1:5).
- He granted us an inheritance (Col. 1:12).
- He delivered us from darkness (Col. 1:13).
- He judges (Heb. 10:30).
- He is love (1 John 4:7–8).

In the book of Isaiah, chapters 61 and 62 paint a beautiful picture of the year of the Lord's favor, but chapter 63 turns a corner in describing the day of the Lord's wrath. However, Isaiah gives us some helpful tools for understanding how these things fit together in God's personality. He uses specific terminology to show how God's goodness far outweighs His wrath. For instance, compare the day of His wrath to the year of His favor and redemption (Isa. 61:2; 63:4). That's 365 times more favor than wrath!

Many scholars say Exodus 34:6–7 is the most quoted verse within the Bible itself.[6] In the passage, God described

Himself to Moses—who He is and what He's like. It paints such a detailed, succinct picture of God—compassionate, gracious, slow to anger, and so forth. Also, God says He keeps faithful love for a thousand generations, but He only punishes to the third or fourth generation.

I wonder if it's possible that the specific order God used to describe Himself carries meaning. Sort of like food labels. When it comes to ingredients, the FDA requires manufacturers to list them in order of predominance.[7] Whatever ingredient is listed first is used in the greatest amount, and the following ingredients are being used in lesser amounts. He begins by describing Himself with traits we would most easily identify as beautiful—merciful, gracious, slow to anger, abounding in love—then He moves to the things we'd be less likely to deem desirable—punishing iniquity and rebellion and sin.

He knows we struggle with the idea of wrath. But despite how it makes us bristle, wrath is not the ugly underbelly of God. Even His wrath is praiseworthy. How so? We don't trust people who dismiss evil as "no big deal." Sin has to be punished. When we see wickedness in the world, we want it to be stopped, and we long for justice to be done. We can be comforted to know it's all handled by our loving Father, who is both righteous and good.

By the math of Exodus 34 and Isaiah 61–63, it seems God is trying to communicate something to us about His character. Perhaps He's approximately three hundred times more loving.

Perhaps He's three hundred times more favorful. Probably these are just generalities that don't quite fit on a precise scale. Regardless of how the math works out, it seems God wants to be known for who He really is—a benevolent God full of mercy and grace.

In addition to that, it's important to recognize how God lovingly and righteously handles the sins of His kids. If we don't understand the dynamics of our relationship with the Father, there's a good chance we will view Him wrongly when we sin. **Our relationship with God the Father changed when He became *our* Father, not just *the* Father**—which happened as a result of our faith in Jesus.

When we surrender to the reality that we can't save ourselves, and we embrace the truth that Jesus was the only perfect sacrifice to cover our sin debt, then God's response to our sin shifts. We're no longer punished for our sins because Jesus took our punishment. If you're a child of God, that means **you will never face God's wrath. Never.** Consider the truth of John 3:36: "Whoever believes in the Son has eternal life; whoever does not obey the Son shall not see life, but the wrath of God remains on him." Wrath remains on the person who does not believe in the Son and does not obey Him. If you're in Christ, then this verse doesn't apply to you! No wrath is left for your sin because Christ absorbed it all on the cross. You won't face God's wrath in this life or in eternity, or even when you stumble and fall in this life, because Christ absorbed all the Father's wrath for your sins—past, present, and future—on the cross. His death covers all your sins, and more than that, His righteousness has been assigned to you!

This doesn't mean God isn't grieved by your sins or that He doesn't discipline you into greater holiness, but remember: **Christian discipline is training, not punishment.** That also doesn't mean our sins don't impact us or those around us— they absolutely do. But it's helpful to understand how God views the sins of His children because that equips us to run *toward* Him when we sin, not *away* from Him.

After humanity fell, Adam and Eve hid from God. They ran from Him. And what did God do? He sought them out, even called them out of their hiding with a question. Imagine that. God coaxes us out of hiding in order to have a conversation with us about what happened. He doesn't avoid us. Then He sacrificed an animal to cover their nakedness and shame (a foretaste of the sacrifice of Christ which would cover our sin and shame too), all before they got expelled from the garden. And even after they were expelled, God didn't stay in the garden; He went with them into exile and through the desert. He never left them, even in their waywardness.

We see this theme repeated throughout Scripture: God moves toward His kids when we struggle, not away. When the Israelites were in the wilderness for forty years sinning against Him and forgetting Him, God decided to dwell in the midst of them. Then He moved them into the promised land and told them to come *into His courts* when they sin, to offer their sacrifices there. He literally told them to come *nearer* when they sinned. Years later, when they were driven into exile because of their great wickedness, God's presence left His temple and went with them into exile in a foreign land.

From the beginning of humanity, just as Adam and Eve did, we've been running from God when we sin. We run and try to hide. But He invites us to draw near. God isn't afraid of your sin, as if sin could beat Him or overcome Him. God isn't afraid of anything. Everything that isn't God is less than perfect, so He's used to it. If it were possible for God to be corrupted by our sin, He'd have to stay quarantined by Himself, away from all of us forever. Yet never once did He look at His kids and say, "You guys are really messing things up. I'm going to an island in the Bahamas until you figure this out." No. He entered in, He moved *toward us* in our misery because He knows sinners can't fix themselves. We would have no hope of being clean without Him!

But to be clear: He tells *us* to run from sin because we *can* be corrupted by it—He can't but we can.

Not only is God unafraid of your sin, but He is not shocked by it either. How is that possible? In order to be shocked or disappointed, you have to have an expectation that is unmet, but God has no unmet expectations of you. You sin exactly the number of times He knows you will. That's one of the perks of being omniscient and being outside of time: He knows everything! He knows all the sins you've committed, the ones you're still struggling with and fighting against even now, and all the times you'll lose that battle in the future. He knows. You, on the other hand, may be surprised and shocked at your sin, but He isn't. Now, don't get me wrong. He's grieved by it. He aches over it. And at the same time, He provides for you in it with the riches of the gospel. He draws near to you in it. To heal you.

Child of God, you are being conformed to the image of Christ, day by day, by the work of His Spirit in you. He is patient with you as He's working in you. Our salvation starts with the Father (John 6:33). Jesus says we have to hear and learn from the Father and that the Father is the one who draws us (John 6:44–45). Other Scriptures we'll encounter reveal that He uses the Spirit as a means of drawing us, just as the Son is the means of redeeming us—but it all starts with the Father's plan, and He's working it out through each Person of the Trinity. And remember: **what the Father initiates, He will sustain, and He will fulfill** (Phil. 1:6).

He's a Father worth loving and worshipping. Not only that, but He's actually pretty amazing to be around. He's not a drag; He's a delight! He's not looking to smite everyone who defies Him (or else we'd all be annihilated by now). In fact, He's already made a way to completely bridge the gap between His holiness and our sinfulness so we can just enjoy Him! After all, He's where the joy is!

3

God the Son

Three Foundations of the Trinity

1. There is only one true God.

2. There are three divine Persons of the one true God.

3. The three Persons are co-equal,
co-eternal, and co-relational.

Who Is the Son?

The second Person of the Trinity is God the Son. He is the Son because He is eternally begotten of the Father, and His eternality means He isn't younger than the Father. They both exist eternally. God the Son doesn't just reveal Himself to creation—He actually reveals the Father to creation as well,

and the Son does it in a way that is unique to Him. While
God the Father is spirit, God the Son is connected with the
physical aspects of creation. We'll study some of the specifics
of His relationship with creation throughout this chapter.

Being the Son makes Him no less God than the Father.
Our finite capacity for eternal things makes it difficult for us
to grasp how the Father didn't create the Son and that they're
both eternal. After all, we've seen family trees and genealogies,
and we know how time works. But in order to even scratch the
surface of this, we have to detach ourselves from our earthly
understanding of time. As the third foundation of the Trinity
reminds us, the Father and Son (and Spirit) are co-eternal.
But instead of just taking that as fact and nodding our heads,
let's dig into Scripture to see what truths helped theologians
clarify these foundations over the years.

While the foundations of the Trinity were a regular part
of the conversation among the early church, they have flown
under the radar so long for us that we barely notice them when
we read Scripture. Before we move into the New Testament
writings about the Son, let's look at some Old Testament hints
that reveal who He is.

The first passage we'll spend some time exploring is Psalm
110:1:

> The LORD says to my **Lord**: "Sit at my right
> hand, until I make your enemies your foot-
> stool." (emphasis added)

This prophetic psalm is the most frequently quoted Old Testament verse in the New Testament, which tells us the early church regarded it as necessary and foundational.[1] This particular verse has two uses of the word *Lord*, and it's important to note that they're written differently. (Notice how the first instance appears in all caps, and the second instance has only the first letter capitalized.)

In the original language, these two instances are two different words with two different functions and meanings. In Hebrew, a language that doesn't use vowels, the name of God was written as "YHWH." Out of reverence, many Jews won't speak it, but others pronounce it as "Yahweh" or "Jehovah." It's most often translated in Scripture as LORD (all caps), and we regard it as God's personal name. His title, on the other hand, is the word *Adonai* in Hebrew, and it means "Master or Lord." It's most often translated as *Lord*.[2] Psalm 110:1 may seem peculiar when we first read the English translation, but this information about "LORD" and "Lord" helps us clarify the meaning of the verse. And since both words (*LORD, Lord*) can be used to refer to any person of the Trinity, this verse offers us some help in understanding what David was communicating in this passage via the Spirit's guidance (Matt. 22:43).

Bear with me because a lot of **theology** is packed into this tiny verse! King David wrote this psalm thousands of years before God the Son came to live on earth. David said the LORD said to his Lord, "Sit at my right hand." At least a dozen New Testament verses refer to the Son's being seated at the right hand of the Father. But those New Testament verses hadn't been written when David wrote this psalm. Still he referred to the Son as his "Lord," the One seated at the right hand of the Father.

In short, this verse is where David overheard God the Father talking to God the Son. David's Lord is God the Son, who had not yet been born into His earthly position but who has always existed nonetheless.

Eternality

No one made the Son. This is challenging for our brains because we're confined to time, but in the realm of eternity and an eternal triune God, the Son is not younger than the Father. He is, as Scripture and the creeds say, "eternally begotten."[3]

We don't use the word *beget* much in modern language, but the general idea refers to becoming the father of something that is of your own kind. It's unlike creating, which points to something different from yourself. Scripture calls Jesus the "only begotten" Son of the Father (John 1:14; 3:16 KJV). Since the Father has been fathering eternally, before time, then His Son is eternally begotten and has no point of origin.

Several Scriptures help us gain greater clarity on the eternality of God the Son, including the words of Jesus Himself in John 8:58, "Truly, truly, I say to you, before Abraham was, I am." Not only was He saying He predated Abraham, but He was using the name of God ("I AM," Exod. 3:14) as His identifier. He also refers to Himself as the first and last

(Rev. 1:17–18) and the Alpha and Omega, the beginning and the end (Rev. 22:13).

The theologians of the early church worked hard to clarify this point, shaping their language precisely in the Nicene Creed: "We believe in one Lord, Jesus Christ, the only Son of God, eternally begotten of the Father, God from God, Light from Light, true God from true God, begotten not made, one in being with the Father."[4] I certainly can't say it better or more clearly than that.

Creator

The Son is the only begotten of the Father, beloved of the Father. He is the Word (*Logos*).[5] He is light. He has always been all those things. As we discussed in the chapter about God the Father, God's "being" and "doing" are interwoven, so He always acts out of who He is. As a result, we'll see lots of overlap once again as we aim to dissect the way the Son engages with His creation.

Not only did no one create God the Son, but in fact, He is the one who created all things. Said another way, **the Son wasn't part of what God created; He was within the Godhead, creating**. He has always existed as God the Son. John 1:3 says, "All things were made through him and without him was not any thing made that was made." Colossians 1:16 reiterates this, "For by him all things were created, in heaven and on earth, visible and invisible, whether thrones or dominions or rulers or authorities—all things were created through him and for him." God the Father commanded creation, God the Son fulfilled the manual labor of creating, and God the Spirit approved of and sustained it. The Trinity—the three Persons of the One true God—has always existed in total unity, working together toward the same goal.

All things were created through God the Son. He built the things the Father spoke into existence with His creation command, showing us once again His unique relationship to the physical realm. It's like the Father was the architect of creation, with Jesus bringing those plans into existence.[6] But then Jesus stepped through eternity and into time to live in the world He built. He also eternally inherits it all (Heb. 1:2). The only reason the Son is the Son on earth is because He is the Son in eternity. And in order for Him to be God the eternal Son, He must have always existed. To have always existed is to be without a Creator.

Theophanies

Throughout the Old Testament, we find other breadcrumbs that point us toward God the Son. While God the Father is spirit and has no physical form, God the Son, even in the Old Testament, has some unique connections to the physical realm. Because of this, the Son is often attributed with many of the **theophanies** in Scripture. A theophany is any appearance of God in Scripture that humans could perceive with their senses. A **Christophany** is a theophany of Christ specifically.

In some theophanies, God appeared in a form that was visible yet nonhuman. For instance, one of the most memorable theophanies in Scripture is when God appeared to Moses at the burning bush (Exod. 3). When He was with the Israelites in the wilderness, He not only appeared as a pillar of fire but also as a pillar of cloud (Exod. 33:9–11; Deut. 31:15). He appeared to Job in a whirlwind (Job 38:1). Some people believe these examples were God the Father taking on an earthly or visible form. Others believe that since humans can't see God and live (Exod. 33:20; John 5:37; 6:46), these appearances are actually Christophanies—an appearance connected with God the Son instead of the Father.[7]

Unlike the fire, cloud, and wind appearances, Scripture describes other theophanies when God appears in a form that is described as human or at least includes the element of personhood (Gen. 18:1–2; 32:24–30; Josh. 5:13–15). When theophanies correspond to a human figure, some verses clarify that God is the One appearing (Gen. 22:15–18; Exod. 3:2–4), and other verses refer to the being as "the angel of the LORD" (Judg. 6:22; Zech. 1:11–13). But who is "the angel of the LORD"? Three things are worth noting as we seek to answer this question.

1. The Hebrew word for *angel* means "messenger" and doesn't refer exclusively to a type of created being.[8] When angels appear in Scripture, they always appear as or resemble men though they aren't human; they're an entirely different order of created beings, and they are not made in the image of God.

2. Scripture seems to mark out a distinction between "the" angel of the LORD and "an" angel of the LORD. The appearances recognized as theophanies use the terminology ***the angel of the LORD***. Whereas most scholars consider appearances describing the spiritual visitor as ***an angel of the LORD*** to be the created heavenly being.

3. In these theophanies, the being says or does something only God could claim or do. For example:

- The angel of the LORD claims to have the power of life and death as seen in Genesis 16:10 (csb): "The angel of the LORD said to her, 'I will greatly multiply your offspring, and they will be too many to count.'" (See also 2 Kings 19:3: "That night the angel of the LORD went out and struck down 185,000 in the camp of the Assyrians."

- The theophanic being also receives worship, as in Joshua 5:13–15: "A man was standing before him with his drawn sword in his hand. . . . And he said, '. . . I am the commander of the army of the LORD. . . .' And Joshua fell on his face to the earth and worshiped. . . . And the commander of the LORD's army said to Joshua, 'Take off your sandals from your feet, for the place where

you are standing is holy.' And Joshua did
so."

- The "angel of the LORD" delivered them out
  of slavery, brought them into the promised
  land, and made a covenant with them, as
  seen in Judges 2:1–5 (CSB): "The angel of
  the LORD went up from Gilgal to Bochim
  and said, 'I brought you out of Egypt and
  led you into the land I had promised to
  your ancestors. I also said: I will never
  break my covenant with you. You are not
  to make a covenant with the inhabitants of
  this land. You are to tear down their altars.
  But you have not obeyed me. What have
  you done? Therefore, I now say: I will not
  drive out these people before you. They
  will be thorns in your sides, and their gods
  will be a trap for you.' When the angel of
  the LORD had spoken these words to all
  the Israelites, the people wept loudly. So
  they named that place Bochim and offered
  sacrifices there to the LORD."

- (For more interesting interactions, explore
  passages like Judges 6:11–18; 2 Kings
  19:33–35; and Job 38:1–3.)

None of this means that God the Son was an angel, nor
does it mean He was a man—at least not yet. As John Owen

described it, "He was as yet God only; but appeared in the assumed shape of a man, to signify what he would be. He did not create a human nature, and unite it unto himself for such a season; only by his divine power he acted the shape of a man composed of what ethereal substance he pleased, immediately to be dissolved. So he appeared to Abraham, to Jacob, to Moses, to Joshua, and others."[9]

God the Son's role in connecting with humanity has always had a unique physical element to it, which is one reason many theologians believe these appearances could uniquely pertain to God the Son. Another reason is that these unique appearances cease after God the Son comes to earth as the fully God, fully man Messiah. (Note: *An* angel of the Lord appears after that point but never *the* angel of the Lord.) As with the Trinity, we gain a clearer understanding of these Old Testament appearances in the New Testament. Whether these were preincarnate appearances of God the Son or not, the full revealing of the Messiah and His life, death, and resurrection were still necessary for the completion of God's redemption story.

Prophecies

The Old Testament also points to Jesus in other ways—namely, prophecies. Jesus said the Old Testament is about Him (John 5:39–40). He is all over its pages in theophanies, prophecies, pictures, and archetypes of Him. Even though the Old Testament doesn't fully reveal the Trinity, it effectively drops the breadcrumbs for us so we can see the path as we look back. Step-by-step, it leads us closer to the fulfillment of the promise of the Messiah and the revelation that the Messiah is God Himself.

Most scholars say Genesis 3:15 is the first prophecy about Jesus in Scripture. It talks about His victory over the enemy. ("He shall bruise your head, and you shall bruise his heel.") But I'm inclined to think the first prophecy of the coming Messiah may have happened in Genesis 1:3 where we see the first recorded words of God speaking. In this verse, God looked out over the dark chaotic world, knowing all the brokenness that was about to take place after He finished creating it—all the sin and pain and wickedness—and said, "Let there be light." I wonder if that's more than just a creation command. I wonder if it's a promise—almost like He's saying, "Things are about to get very dark, but hold on. Light is coming. He's coming." If that is in fact a prophecy, Jesus is certainly the fulfillment of it. After all, John says of Christ: "In him was life, and that life was the light of men. That light shines in the darkness, and yet the darkness did not overcome it.... The ... only Son of God ... the light has come into the world" (John 1:4–5; 3:18–19 csb). And if that's not enough, Jesus calls Himself "the light of the world" three times (John 8:12; 9:5; 12:46)!

Most prophecies provide us with a greater sense of clarity but often only because we have the benefit of hindsight. At the time the prophecies were originally given, most of the people who heard or read the words of the prophets could not have known exactly how those prophecies might be fulfilled. For instance, when the Old Testament prophets spoke of a coming King, most people expected an earthly ruler who would save them from their oppressive rulers. In New Testament times, many of the Jewish people hoped and expected that the coming Messiah would overthrow the oppressive Roman government.[10] Their minds couldn't conceive what God was really promising: a divine Ruler who would reign over an eternal kingdom.

Similarly, when Jesus talked to His disciples, He sometimes spoke clearly about future things, but they still didn't understand. For instance, He repeatedly told them things like, "I'm going to die, and then I'll rise again three days later" (Mark 9:30–31), but no one understood His words until after He fulfilled them.

Because of the way God works through **progressive revelation**, it seems like He intended to drop some prophetic breadcrumbs without a full explanation of where they were leading. With our current, fuller view of the story, it's helpful to read the Old Testament in light of the New Testament, and vice versa, in order to see a clearer picture of what God has revealed about God the Son.

The Son in His Incarnation

One thing I've found helpful in studying the Trinity is to delineate between the terms "God the Son" and "Jesus." They are the same person, of course, but the distinction serves us in two different ways. First, it reminds us that God the Son has always existed. Second, it reminds us that in eternity past and up until His incarnation, the Son had not yet taken on the name or human nature of Jesus.

It's not wrong for us to refer to Him as "Jesus" before His incarnation—and at times it may even be helpful—it's just imprecise. God the Son became human when He was conceived in Mary's womb, and He took on the name *Jesus* when He was born in Bethlehem, but He always has been and always will be God the Son.

While in earlier sections we've already explored Jesus's eternality (meaning He not only predates the creation of the world but has also always existed), it is important and bears repeating. In fact, according to Sanders, Jesus's preexistence is "more foundational than his virgin birth."[11] In other words, it's more important where He came from eternally than where He came from temporally. When we say, "Jesus is preexistent," this means He existed as God the Son before He entered into His creation as a human. His eternal nature has always been because He is the uncreated, eternal God. Then, during His time on earth (and even now), along with His eternal, divine nature, He took on a human nature. Jesus was (and is) both fully God and fully man.

The Right and Only Sufficient Substitute

The New Testament spends a lot of time establishing that Jesus is God. Sometimes Jesus is the one to demonstrate that reality by His own words, in His miracles, or as seen in His resurrection from the dead. In addition to His own testimony, the apostles and the writers of Scripture testified about it as well, and the early church affirmed it.

The books of Romans and Titus both refer to Jesus as God. In Romans 9:5, when Paul is talking about the blessings of the Jews, he says, "To them belong the patriarchs, and from their race, according to the flesh, is *the Christ, who is God over all*, blessed forever" (emphasis added). And in Titus 2:13–14, Paul says we are "waiting for our blessed hope, the appearing of the glory of our *great God and Savior Jesus Christ*, who gave himself for us" (emphasis added).

The New Testament reaffirms the monotheism of the Old Testament (Acts 17:16–34) while also affirming the deity of Jesus. It naturally follows that if there's only one God, and if Jesus is God, then He must be coequal with the Father; otherwise there would be more than one God, and one of them would be dominant over the other, lesser being. But as we've learned, that's not the case. All three Persons are distinct but unified. The book of John also points to this. It refers to Jesus as "the Word," and it says, "The Word was *with* God, and the Word *was* God" (1:1, emphasis added). Jesus is both identified as God and distinguished from God the Father. And later in that same book, Jesus calls Himself "I am" (8:58), which is His way of self-identifying with God. This was no small claim—it was a big enough deal that their response was to try to stone Him.

If Jesus were only partly human, His death wouldn't cover our sin debt (Isa. 53:5; Rom. 5:6–8; 1 Pet. 3:18). We need a fully *human* substitute to overcome a fully *human* problem. Put differently, humans started the problem of sin, and so only a human could finish it. At the same time, if Jesus were only partly God, He wouldn't have been able to live the perfectly righteous life we need Him to live in order to grant it to us (Jer. 33:16; 2 Cor. 5:21; 1 Pet. 2:24). The substitute we needed had to be someone who could live an entire life without sin—and only God is without sin! So we see Jesus must be both fully God and fully man—meaning 100 percent divine and 100 percent human—in order to both pay our sin debt and grant us His righteousness. He is the only possible mediator between us and God the Father. He's the only One who can bridge the gap because He's the only One who has both a fully divine and fully human nature at the same time.

Humans are born into fallenness, brokenness, and our inherent sin nature. We have a sin debt, but we exist in spiritual poverty and can't pay it. We need someone who is spiritually rich to pay our sin debt. But then, even if our debt were paid, we would only be at spiritual "zero"—poor sinners who owe nothing but *have* nothing.

God's great love wasn't content to let us stay that way. He didn't want us to be mere strangers who were no longer in debt to Him; He wanted us to be integrated into His family, adopted into His eternal kingdom of righteousness to live with Him forever. In order for that to happen, we don't just need someone to get us to spiritual "zero." We need someone to get us all the way to spiritual righteousness! Which is why the incarnation is so important. In the person of Christ, God entered into His creation and took on flesh as a human to solve our problem once and for all. In His life and death, Jesus not only *took away* our sin as a *human sacrifice*; He *gave* us His *fully righteous, human record* before the Father—a perfect record we desperately needed to stand on in order to be accepted by God but had no hope of earning ourselves.

By dying for our sins, He could pay the debt we owed. By living the perfect, sinless life, He could grant us His righteousness. (To see a mix of Bible verses that point to either Jesus paying for our sins or Jesus granting us His righteousness, look up Isa. 53:5; Jer. 33:16; Matt. 3:15; Rom. 5:6–8; 2 Cor. 5:21; 1 Pet. 2:24; 3:18.) As it turns out, we don't just need Christ's death; we need His whole life too! And thankfully, by coming to earth and taking on flesh in the incarnation, He gives us this very thing!

Think on this reality for just a little bit longer and really let it sink in. Jesus had to live the perfect life on earth—not just come down to die for us. If we didn't need His perfect life, He could've descended from heaven during Passover, then died and resurrected in three days. He would've been able to avoid all the trials of an earthly life—the temptations in the desert, the death of His friends, being doubted by His family members and betrayed by His disciples. He could have escaped so much additional pain and suffering!

But we needed His life. Without it, our sins would've been paid for by His perfect sacrificial death so we would be sinless before God, but we still wouldn't be righteous. We would be pardoned sinners, not righteous saints. We would be out of spiritual jail, so to speak, but not adopted into the kingdom— and there's no place for that kind of neutrality in God's world. Jesus had to come and live the perfect life, which was then attributed *to us*. By His life, death, resurrection, and ascension, God's kids are afforded not only the payment for their sins but the righteousness of Christ and a shared inheritance in His kingdom.

The Ongoing Impact

His incarnation is still true to this day. Meaning He has a continued incarnation, even now, at the right hand of the Father. His physical state is not one He decided to "divorce from" after He completed the work of the cross and the resurrection. He stayed in His incarnated state for the rest of eternity so He could forever identify with us!

On top of this, His incarnation means we can forever feel understood by Him no matter what temptations and trials we face in our physical and emotional lives (Heb. 4:15). Because Christ chose to be human, He knows exactly what our human experience feels like day in and day out. There's nothing we can go through that He doesn't have compassion for. He knows what it's like to get tired, to cry, to face rejection, to be humiliated physically, to have a broken body, and to experience a full range of human emotions (Heb. 5:2).

In the incarnation we don't just have a Savior who saved us but a Savior who gets us and can sympathize with whatever human struggle or ailment we lift up to Him! His incarnation means that, no matter the situation, you can run to Him because He really does get what it's like to face the hard and human challenges you face every day. Because of His incarnation, it's easy for us to understand what it means to be friends with Him (John 15:15).

The Son in Relationship

John 3:16 is a powerful summary of the gospel, and John 15:13 says Jesus's death demonstrated that He has the greatest kind of love for us. But if we disconnect Jesus's love for us from who He says He is in the rest of Scripture, we miss the point entirely. Why would it matter that Jesus loves us or died for us if He's just a good teacher? If that's all He is, nothing shifts in our lives. My first-grade teacher loved me, and while that was a real confidence booster that shaped me, it didn't alter my eternity. According to Jesus's claims in John 8:24, we will die in our sins unless we believe He is who He says He is.

Since, according to Him, that's so vital, let's look at some of the things He said, did, and claimed about Himself to help us form a better understanding of who He is.

- First, He did things only God can do—He forgave sins (Mark 2:5–7) and raised from the dead (Luke 24:5–7).
- Second, He received worship (Matt. 28:9; John 9:38) and didn't rebuke others for claiming He is God (Matt. 14:33; Luke 22:70; John 20:28).
- Third, He claimed to be one with the Father (John 10:30; 14:8–11; 17:21–22).
- Fourth, He also demonstrated that He is distinct from the Father (John 5:22; 8:48–50; 11:41–42; 14:16; 17:1–5).

Taken altogether, these things demonstrate the unique Father-Son relationship of the Trinity. John 1:1 even marks it out for us: Jesus (who is the Word made flesh) both is God and is with God. United with the Father yet distinct from the Father.

Hypostatic Union

This isn't the only aspect of Jesus's personhood that is united yet distinct. This same concept applies to the way His human nature interacts with His divine nature. Theologians call this concept **hypostatic union**. *Hypostatic* means "personal," and it points to the fact that Jesus is one person, not two people—fully human, fully divine within Himself.[12]

The Council of Chalcedon (AD 451) declared that Jesus is "truly God and truly man" and that His two natures are "without confusion, without change, without division, without separation; the distinction of nature's being in no way annulled by the union."[13] The two natures of Jesus are distinct yet united perfectly. There's a temptation to overlap them, but they can't be blended just as they can't be separated.

As we've said before, Jesus is fully God and fully man. He is not a hybrid of the two because hybrid means "mixture" and there has been no blending of His two natures—He isn't an in-between being like a mermaid or a centaur (neither of which is fully human). There is no dilution of either aspect of who He is because that would mean He would lose the fullness of either His divine or His human nature.

Jesus embodied the qualities of both natures. He grew tired, hungry, and thirsty like every other man (Luke 24:41–42; John 4:6; 19:28). And He raised the dead, could read minds, commanded the weather, and knew the future as only God can do (Matt. 26:21; Mark 2:8; 4:39; John 11:43). Despite how different His two natures are, they aren't separated; in Jesus, they're united. In fact, they're so tightly bound together that He even makes one nature submissive to the other at times, without losing the attributes of either. For instance, He made His human nature submit to His divine nature when He prayed in the garden of Gethsemane on the night before

He died. His human nature wanted to avoid the pain, but His divine nature desired obedience to the Father's plan more than anything else, so His human nature yielded to His divine nature (Matt. 26:39).

The fact that God took on flesh shows us that He is absolutely, unmistakably for us (Rom. 5:8). He released the privileges of His kingship and came to live as a humble servant among us, pouring Himself into flesh (Phil. 2:6–7). He endured great pains to restore you to the Father because there was no other way for it to happen. Jesus's hypostatic union makes Him perfectly and uniquely suited to be our Savior.

Mediator

In order to be our Savior, Jesus can't be 50 percent God and 50 percent man; He must be fully and completely 100 percent both—fully God and fully man. This is why it's impossible for us to find salvation through anyone besides Jesus—He is the only Mediator, the only place where God and man overlap (John 14:6; Acts 4:12). He is the "only begotten Son" (John 3:16 KJV)—the "one of a kind" Son of God—eliminating the possibility of any other mediator.

Consider how these verses reveal the role Jesus plays in our relationship with the Father:

- "For there is one God and one mediator between God and mankind, the man Christ Jesus." (1 Tim. 2:5 CSB)

- "Therefore, he is the mediator of a new covenant, so that those who are called might receive the promise of the eternal inheritance, because a death has taken place for redemption from the transgressions committed under the first covenant." (Heb. 9:15 csb)

We see "mediator" all over these passages, don't we? To summarize R. C. Sproul in *The Work of Christ*, what's remarkable about Jesus isn't that He died on a cross. The Romans crucified thousands of people, perhaps even hundreds of thousands—so that doesn't make Jesus unique. And it wasn't just that He was innocent of what He was accused of; the Romans certainly crucified others who were falsely accused. The uniqueness of Jesus stems solely from His divinity. Being fully God and fully man set Him up to be *the bridge*—the mediator—between God and mankind. Just as someone who speaks two languages can translate between two people who speak different languages, Jesus is the only means we have for communicating with and being in relationship with the Father.[14]

In our relationship with Jesus, we each bring something to the relationship—either sin or righteousness, either the curse of death or the blessing of life. Jesus brings righteousness and life. We bring sin and death. He traded His righteousness for our sin, granting us His righteousness. He traded His life for our death, granting us eternal life (2 Cor. 5:21).

What a great comfort! Knowing that we fall short of God's requirements and have earned the curse of death, we are given an incredible gift that grants Christ's righteousness for free (Rom. 3:21–26; 6:23). Martin Luther reportedly called this the "glorious exchange" where we trade what belongs to us (sin and death) for what belongs to Jesus (righteousness and life).[15] This should set our hearts at ease, knowing that Jesus has accomplished all the Father requires of us.

The Son's Actions

In this section, we'll look at a few of the roles specific to the Son. All of Jesus's actions and interactions on earth point us back to the relational beauty of the Trinity. Nothing He does is intended to put the spotlight on Himself. For example, according to Philippians 2:5–11, we don't see Jesus climbing up some ladder to get attention; rather we see Him lowering Himself, as the text makes clear that He *emptied* Himself and *humbled* Himself (vv. 7–8). As a result, the Father exalted Him (v. 9), and the Father will be glorified when every tongue confesses that Jesus is Lord (vv. 10–11). Do you see it? Jesus doesn't grab at the glory that comes with having "the name above all names"—the *Father* is the one who desires to give such glory to Christ Jesus. And the Father gains glory when people bow to *Christ* to praise Him. There is a reciprocity within the Trinity—they don't seek their own individual glory separate from the others; instead, they point toward one anothers' glory.

The three divine Persons are inseparable in their unified action toward humanity because each divine Person is engaged in the story and work of redemption. As they work together toward their unified goal, they each have unique roles they've chosen to fulfill. Since their nature is unified, their relationships and roles make them distinct. This points back to what we learned about the **Economic Trinity**, the external work of the Godhead as it relates to creation and humanity.

All of the Son's actions are pleasing to the Father. In fact, even before Jesus's ministry began, the Father approved of Him and was pleased with Him (Matt. 3:17). Some of the things we'll look at in this section are things He did before His birth. It bears repeating: God the Son has always existed.

Now, let's look at a few roles and actions we can observe about the Son.

Made a Way for Us

While Jesus was certainly a good moral teacher and a great philosopher and even a good example for us to follow, those things are not the necessary or primary markers of His identity. If those things are all He was, then His death was pointless because He has no power to save. Jesus merely being a good teacher or philosopher would also mean it would be impossible for Him to love you—because He would have stayed dead after his death (and therefore wouldn't know you), because He wouldn't be outside of time (because no mere human is), because He wouldn't be God. But Scripture tells us that because He's God, He has the ability to pray for you even now; that's right, the living and breathing Son of God is talking to the Father about you (Rom. 8:34–35)! Not only does He know you, but as we've said before when exploring His incarnation, He knows what it feels like to be you (Heb. 4:15). All these things taken together mean not only that Jesus is God but that He loves you and understands you unlike anyone else!

So we know that the Son is fully God and that He entered the world in the person of Christ. Then if we fast-forward a bit, we know that He is in heaven now, alive and well, interceding for you. But what happened between the moment He entered the world and the moment He went back to heaven in order to intercede for you? What was He up to? What role or action was He fulfilling? Colossians 1 provides us with a clear answer. As we'll see, it offers a helpful, condensed view of not only who Jesus is, but what He came to do during His earthly ministry:

> He is the image of the invisible God, the first-born of all creation. For by him all things were created, in heaven and on earth, visible and invisible, whether thrones or dominions or rulers or authorities—all things were created through him and for him. And he is before all things, and in him all things hold together.

And he is the head of the body, the church. He is the beginning, the firstborn from the dead, that in everything he might be preeminent. For in him all the fullness of God was pleased to dwell, and through him to **reconcile to himself all things, whether on earth or in heaven, making peace by the blood of his cross.**

And you, who once were alienated and hostile in mind, doing evil deeds, **he has now reconciled in his body of flesh by his death, in order to present you holy and blameless and above reproach before him.** (Col. 1:15–22, emphasis added)

This passage reiterates what we've already discovered in previous sections about Jesus's identity: He is the preexistent image of the invisible God and the Creator of the universe. But pay attention to the bolded parts, which help us see not only His identity but also the role or action He seeks to fulfill: God the Son came to earth to live, die, and raise from the dead with one primary goal in mind—uniting God to His children by the blood of the cross, to the glory of God.

In other words, His earthly ministry was all about making a way for us when there was no other way to be restored to God! He's the connection point—the *only* sufficient and lasting connection point—between humanity and the Father. No one can bridge the gap between a man and God the Father except Jesus, because as we've already noted, He is the only substitutionary candidate who is both fully God and fully man. There is no other way to be restored to the Father; Jesus is the only way because He's the only one qualified for the job. That's precisely why He identifies Himself as "the way" (John 14:6).

C. S. Lewis said that when we're confronted with the statements Jesus made (one of which is His claim that He's the only "way" to God), we're forced to recognize Him as either a lunatic, a liar, or Lord.[16] Either He was crazy for calling Himself such a thing, or He was a liar and knew He was not the Waymaker but still deceptively acted like He was, or He was saying something that really was true—in which case, He truly is the One who made a way to be reconciled to God when there was no other way.

Think about this: if there were any other way for God's kids to be reconciled to Him, then Jesus didn't have to die. If any path to God were sufficient or if we could earn our way into that relationship by being good, then Jesus's death was unnecessary and cruel. He could've been spared all of the pain of His death. But the reason Jesus pressed on, even through the pain He knew He'd endure (John 18:4), is because He knew the truth: there was no other way. We can't fix ourselves. Brokenness can't repair itself to a state of perfection. Our sin debt has to be paid by someone, and Jesus is the only one who could be the perfect sacrifice because only He is perfect. As we've said before, He is the only fully God, fully Man Savior Messiah King. No other bridge to God is as sturdy as that one!

Jesus willingly entered into His assignment—the betrayal, the beatings, the gruesome death, the giving over of His spirit in the last moments of His life. (And for the record, it bears repeating that Jesus emptied and humbled *Himself* in all these agonizing moments. Some outside force wasn't responsible for it. The Father didn't force Him against His will. Jesus did it voluntarily. This helps us see that the Son didn't submit His human will to the Father's plan out of fear of punishment or because He had to; He did it joyfully out of a shared desire and a love for the Father as noted in John 12:49–50 and 14:31. Jesus and the Father wanted the same thing: our rescue! Jesus demonstrated that the Father's heart toward us is for good, for life, for relationship with Himself.) Though His assignment was painful, none of it was in vain, for Revelation 13:8 tells us that Jesus's death on the cross was the plan even before the world was formed. He willingly died this death in order to pay our sin debt. He made a way for us, at the expense of His own life. What a loving, generous God.

Resurrected

So we've covered one of the actions of the Son: making a way for sinful humanity to be restored to the Father through the blood of the cross. But what action can we observe about God the Son *after* the cross? Three days after His death, Jesus rose from the grave. When Mary saw the resurrected Christ, He spoke her name, "Mary" (John 20:16). Weeping, she grabbed onto Him (20:13, 17). When the disciples followed shortly after, they fell at His feet and worshipped Him (Matt. 28:9). There are a few noteworthy things here: First, Jesus receives worship. He knows He is God. Second, they grabbed His *feet*. He's not an apparition or a ghost. He appears in a real, physical, risen body. Third, in ancient times, women couldn't even be witnesses in court. They were considered unreliable. If someone were fabricating this story, they would've chosen a more reliable first witness to help give their tale more validity. But Jesus has always revealed Himself to the rejected and the outcast, to those considered less-than. So it's no surprise that His first resurrected revealing was to a woman—much less one who had once, before her healing and restoration, been possessed by seven demons (Luke 8:2)!

Later that day, the disciples were gathered together, and Jesus appeared in the room with them (Luke 24:36–37). He showed them the holes in His hands and side (24:39–40), and He even asked for food (24:41–43), proving that He wasn't just an apparition. He was flesh and blood raised from the dead. Then He commissioned them to spread the word to the world (24:45–48) and told them to receive the Holy Spirit (24:49).

Why does all this matter? Why is the physical resurrection of Jesus so important? There are many reasons, but I'll give you three. One, if Jesus had simply died and did not resurrect, He'd be on par with every other religious leader in the world—the ones who may have lived moral lives or taught helpful things but whose bones still lie in the grave. Jesus is unlike them precisely because He's the only one who got out of His grave. This is one reason He's superior to all other kinds of rulers, leaders, teachers, or sages. No one else walked out of their own grave like Jesus did! He proved Himself not just a wise sage but the Lord of Life, the Creator whose breath imparts life to our mortal bodies. Two, if Jesus didn't resurrect, it would be clear that He's not strong enough to undo the curse of death that descended on the earth in Genesis 3. We needed a Savior who could reverse the curse—who could undo not just sin itself but the greatest effect of sin, which is death. If Jesus didn't resurrect, our greatest enemy would remain unconquered, and we'd be destined to live in a world that could never escape its greatest curse. Sin, sickness, disease, illness, broken bodies, decay, and death would be the way of things forever, with no shot at a cure. And three, if Jesus didn't resurrect, then *we* have no hope of resurrecting. We are united to Him—what goes for Him goes for us. Because Jesus's body was raised, so will ours! Without His resurrection, we have no hope of physical life after death, nor does the whole world have the hope of being set right again or regenerated. His bodily resurrection is the "firstfruits" (1 Cor. 15:20); it's the start of many more bodily resurrections to come at the end of this fallen world's story, and it's also the firstfruit that points to a fully regenerated world.

Thankfully, the resurrection is true! In the resurrection of Jesus, we see that He *is* indeed the Lord of Life, that He *has* overcome our greatest curse, and that we have the hope of joining Him in resurrection life where we'll live on a fully restored, renewed, and regenerated earth that carries no trace of sin or death!

All of this is why in Paul's first letter to the Corinthians, he said, "If Christ has not been raised, then our preaching is in vain and your faith is in vain" (1 Cor. 15:14). In addition to that, Paul says that if Christ had not been raised, "you are still in your sins" with no hope of redemption, and that if the resurrection wasn't real, Christians who have died have not gone into glory but rather "have perished" (1 Cor. 15:18). His conclusion is spot-on: "If in Christ we have hope in this life only, we are of all people most to be pitied" (1 Cor. 15:19).

Of all the actions of God the Son, His resurrection is the hinge point of history and the foundation of our faith. It's impossible to overemphasize the importance of this event.

Promised the Spirit

In a statement that was likely confusing to His followers at the time, Jesus promised to give His Spirit to all who believed in Him (John 16:7). God the Spirit has always existed, and we see Him throughout Scripture, starting in Genesis 1:2. Jesus said that when He went away after His resurrection, it would actually be better for His followers because that would usher in the next part of God's plan, which involved the Spirit's dwelling in them, empowering them for mission, producing spiritual fruit in them, convicting them, guiding them into truth, sealing them, interceding for them, never leaving them, and so on. We'll take a closer look at the person and work of God the Spirit in the next chapter.

Ascension

Forty days after His resurrection, Jesus walked to the village of Bethany, just outside Jerusalem on the Mount of Olives, and ascended to heaven (Acts 1:9–10). What does this action mean in terms of His overall ministry? The moment of the ascension is the moment Jesus is exalted to supreme authority over the earth (as He literally rises *above* the earth instead of walking on it). As He rises above the world but below heaven, His ascension is also a moment that points to His role as mediator between God and man, heaven and earth.[17] After Christ ascended and fully entered the heavenly realm, He sat down at the right hand of the Father (Acts 7:55–56; Rom. 8:34), where He intercedes for us until He returns. Until then, we rest in His intercession for us, and we hold on tight to the fact that He has *promised* to return for His people (John 14:3; Acts 1:11). The book of Revelation ends with repeated promises that He is coming back soon (Rev. 22:7, 12, 20). (Want some fun theology trivia? Theologians mark these three phases by calling them the *ascension* of Christ, followed by the *session* of Christ, followed by the *return* or *parousia* of Christ.)

Summary of His Actions

Colossians 1:15 says Jesus is the image of the invisible God. In other words, while God is spirit (John 4:24), Jesus is the physical, living, breathing, walking image of this invisible God. Jesus took on flesh and made God's character and personality visible for us. Because God the Son took on a human nature, we can now see God in the face of Jesus Christ. That is the beauty of the incarnation.

But Christ didn't come to show that He could become an incarnated human as some sort of flashy entertainment stunt or trick. No, His incarnation had a purpose. While Jesus did set an example for us to follow (1 Pet. 2:21), much of what He did in the flesh is impossible for us because we aren't divine. I can't build the universe, you can't serve as the mediator between God and man to absorb His wrath on behalf of all His kids, and neither of us can raise ourselves from the dead. On a basic level, we even struggle to put our flesh and sin to death daily (Rom. 7:15–20).

Jesus didn't come just to set a good example for us so that we can get our act together and be acceptable to God. In fact, He came because we can't do those things. We can't live up to His standard. And so the first action associated with His incarnation is that He took on a human nature in order to save you from your own failures! If you have exhausted yourself trying to earn God's favor, you are free to stop striving and rest in the fact that not only did Jesus take on all the Father's wrath toward your sins, but His righteousness has been credited to your account too. That was the heart of His ministry and His actions—to "give his life as a ransom for many" (Mark 10:45). As we've said before, He's not just a good teacher. He's so much more than just a moral example for us to follow. He's our complete and utter rescue! He's the deep exhale of complete acceptance and love, despite all our past and future failings (Rom. 8:1).

In His life, death, burial, and resurrection, Jesus has fulfilled all the Father requires of us (John 19:28–30), and He even took out our worst enemy: death. This proves He is not only the righteous One but the Lord of Life! After fulfilling this, He rose in His ascension, conveying His rulership over the earth, and then He sat down at the right hand of the Father to intercede for us until He returns. As we think on His life and actions, we know there is freedom and joy in living the kind of obedient life He lives, but we can't do it alone. And so Jesus also sent His Spirit to live in us, to empower and direct us to that end! He didn't leave us alone; He sent the Helper (John 14:16), the Spirit. Because God the Son became human and because we are alive in Him, we can participate in life with God! We are united with Him and the Father by the work of the Spirit. We'll read about the Spirit and His role in the next chapter. He's the One who sustains the Father's work in us, moving us deeper into joy with every step. He's where the joy is!

4

God the Spirit

Three Foundations of the Trinity

1. There is only one true God.
2. There are three divine Persons of the one true God.
3. The three Persons are co-equal,
   co-eternal, and co-relational.

Who Is the Spirit?

While the Trinity as a whole can be confusing, we often encounter added confusion when it comes to understanding one Person of God in particular. God the Spirit is often primarily associated with inexplicable behavior—things we don't see or can't understand. Perhaps our lack of knowledge of Him contributes to His being the Person many Christians are least likely to think about or talk about. None of that comes as a surprise, however—just like with each other Person of the Trinity, He doesn't point primarily to Himself, rather to the other Persons of the Godhead. He's focused *outward* instead of self-ward.

But who is He? Is He the Ghost of Jesus left behind on earth after Jesus disappeared? Is He just a force? Does He have a body? Why do we need Him? What is He doing?

God the Spirit is the third Person of the Trinity. But being third doesn't make Him less important or younger than the Father and Son. Like the other two Persons of the Trinity, the Spirit has always existed. He wasn't created after the Son ascended to heaven. He was there even in Genesis 1, hovering over the waters, approving of and affirming the work. More than that, He was there before the creation of the world, just as the Father and the Son were. While God the Son has a unique connection to the created realm through the incarnation, God the Father is spirit (John 4:24), and God the Spirit is spirit too—and this is important. It impacts the way the Father and Spirit relate to each other and to us as well.

"He," Not "It"

Being God the Spirit makes Him no less God than the Father. He's neither a diluted version of the Father nor the concentration of the Father's power—He's a "he," not an "it." He's not a force or an inanimate power source; rather, He's a

Person. In fact, Matthew 28:19 says He shares a name with the Father and the Son; they could never share their name and oneness with a non-person.

After Jesus's death and resurrection, He remained on earth for forty days. Before He ascended back to be with the Father in heaven, He made a promise to pray to the Father and ask Him to send His Spirit to be with His people forever (John 14:16). His prayer reiterates that Father, Son, and Spirit are all distinct Persons united in their being and shared mission. Jesus said it was to His disciples' advantage that He would leave and send the Spirit. He said the Spirit would come and flow from people's hearts like living water. His followers couldn't make sense of His words at the time, but He was setting them up to understand retrospectively.

In the book of Acts, a magician named Simon saw the power of the Spirit at work and wanted that power for himself. He didn't want the Spirit as a Person—he just wanted the Spirit's *power*—and Paul rebuked him for it (Acts 8:9–24). This Spirit is not some*thing* we use to enforce our own agenda, He's some*one* who works in us to accomplish His agenda—to conform us to the image of the Son (Rom. 8:29; 2 Cor. 3:18; Col. 3:10; Phil. 3:21). He shares that goal with the Father and the Son.

Through His work in us, we become the way the world sees what God is like. We extend His love and peace and truth and generosity to the world around us. It's important to remember how the **Economic Trinity** works, the way the triune God interacts with His people. Just as we saw with Jesus, the Spirit submits to the Father's plan—not out of fear of punishment or simply because He has to but because they share a common goal.

The Three work in perfect unity while walking out their specific roles in creation, salvation, and restoration. All those things are fully accomplished by the three Persons of the triune God. What a relief that God accomplishes for us all that God requires of us! **He does the doing.**

But how do we know the Spirit isn't merely a force Jesus used—like His miraculous power? Several passages of Scripture indicate His *personhood*. Jesus called Him the Helper (John 14:16), Isaiah said He is grieved by our sins (Isa. 63:10), Luke said He gives directions for the steps of His people (Acts 8:29; 10:19–20; 13:2), and Paul said He helps us in our weakness by interceding for us (Rom. 8:26) and He grieves over and fights against our efforts to sin (Eph. 4:30).

These verses reveal that the Spirit is a Person, not a force. Jesus refers to the Spirit as the Comforter (John 14:26 KJV), not the comfort. The Spirit isn't merely a feeling. In fact, He has feelings. He is deeply, emotionally connected to us. But it would be a mistake to think He is emotional in the same way we are. Our emotions are influenced by our sin nature, so they may be tangled up with sinful motives, but His nature is perfect and so are His emotions. He is grieved by our sin and rebellion, and He groans for us in prayer. We have to be careful not to describe the Spirit using utilitarian language. He's not some impersonal power source we can tap into at our own whims.

The Spirit is a Person who speaks, comforts, guides, takes action, and has a personality. But how do we know that Person is God? Paul said that no one knows the mind of God except the Spirit of God, who reveals it to us (1 Cor. 2:10–11). And if He knows the mind of God, then He knows all things, making Him omniscient. Psalm 139:7–8 reveals He is omnipresent—everywhere at all times. Hebrews 9:14 testifies to His eternality, and Genesis 1:2 says He was there in the beginning, hovering over the waters at creation. As we've noted before, He wasn't created. John 15:26 tells us that, contrary to being created by the Father, He proceeds from the Father. In fact, this is one of the chief ways we can describe Him within the Trinity—"the One who proceeds."

As the Spirit proceeds from the Father—and some say He proceeds from the Son as well (John 16:7)—He also declares the truths of Jesus (John 16:13–14). If these connections to the Persons and mission of the Father and Son weren't enough to convince us that the Holy Spirit is God, Scripture makes it clear in the story of Ananias as seen in Acts 5:3–4:

> Peter said, "Ananias, why has Satan filled your heart to **lie to the Holy Spirit** and to keep back for yourself part of the proceeds of the land? While it remained unsold, did it not remain your own? And after it was sold, was it not at your disposal? Why is it that you

have contrived this deed in your heart? **You have not lied to man but to God**." (emphasis added)

Do you see it? Here we have Scripture clearly equating lying to the Holy Spirit with lying to God, plain as day! And that's because the Holy Spirit is God, just as the Father is God and the Son is God.

Uniqueness

As God, the Spirit shares the same purpose and goal as the Father and Son. They are eternally united. But let's look at His uniqueness more closely. The first time we see God the Spirit in Scripture is in Genesis 1:2. He made several appearances in the Old Testament and during the ministry of Jesus in the Gospels, but the bulk of His activity in Scripture occurs after Jesus ascended to the Father (Acts 1:6–11). The Scriptures referencing Him were written over the course of hundreds of years by dozens of human authors, but they all tell a consistent and unique story about Him, weaving an interesting thread through their descriptions of Him and His work.

In fact, a consistent motif is represented in several of the passages that speak to His activity: movement in and through the air. In Genesis 1:2, He was hovering over the face of the waters. In Matthew 3:16, His motion descending to rest on Jesus is compared to a dove. In John 3:8, Jesus described His actions as being like the wind. In Acts 2:1–4, Luke said He filled the room "like a mighty rushing wind."

From the beginning, the Spirit is connected to, hovering over, and approving of the work of the Father and the Son. He's associated with wind, and the nature of His presence is to fill things in a way similar to air. Two of the primary words used to describe Him in both the Old and New Testaments (*ruach*,[1] *pneuma*[2]) are closely related to breath and life.

The parallel accounts of the Trinity's activity in both creation and the baptism of Jesus show us their fixed roles. In both events, God the Father was speaking; God the Son was doing; and God the Spirit acted as a hovering seal of approval, enlivening the work. How beautiful! And they use the same pattern in our salvation. God the Father calls us into His family (John 6:37–39); God the Son secures our salvation through His finished work on the cross (John 19:28–30); God the Spirit breathes new life into us and is the seal of our salvation (Eph. 1:13–14).

The Spirit in Relationship with the Trinity

The Father, Son, and Spirit work in perfect unity through their specific roles in creation, salvation, and restoration to bring about the fulfillment of God's eternal plan. Throughout Scripture, we see that the Father initiates all divine action, but He doesn't fulfill or sustain it. The Son is the One who accomplished our salvation, but He didn't author it. And the

Spirit didn't author it either, but He's the one who applies it. The work of our creation, salvation, and restoration is fully accomplished by the three Persons of the triune God. What a RESCUE they've given us! What a relief to know we're not responsible to save ourselves or to sustain our salvation. When we understand the roles the Trinity plays in our rescue, this incredible truth sets our hearts at ease and bears repeating: He does the doing. What God initiates, He will sustain, and He will fulfill.

James B. Torrance described his salvation like this:

> Firstly, I have been a child of God from all eternity in the heart of the Father. Secondly, I became a child of God when Christ the Son lived, died and rose again for me long ago. Thirdly, I became a child of God when the Holy Spirit—the Spirit of adoption—sealed in my faith and experience what had been planned from all eternity in the heart of the Father and what was completed once and for all in Jesus Christ. There are three moments but only one act of salvation, just as we believe there are three persons in the Trinity, but only one God.[3]

Even in the Old Testament, the Father spoke of how the Son and the Spirit are involved in the story of redemption—"I will put my Spirit on him [Jesus]" (Isa. 42:1 NIV). This was fulfilled at Jesus's baptism, when the Spirit visibly descended on Jesus in His fluttering, dovelike way. Later, when Jesus instructed the disciples on baptism, He connected it back to all three Persons of the Trinity as well. He said to baptize in the name—not names—of the Father, Son, and Spirit (Matt. 28:19). Jesus underscored the doctrine of the Trinity in this passage, showing their unity by the use of the singular name and showing their diversity by the specific references. It's significant that Jesus's instructions referenced not only Himself, but the Father and Spirit too. They're all involved uniquely and unitedly.

Everything the Spirit does is connected with the Father and the Son. His work echoes outward, pointing to the other Persons of the Trinity—just as they all do for each other in all things. For instance, everything Jesus did during His time on earth was done by the power of the Spirit. Here are some clear examples:

- Jesus was conceived by the Spirit (Matt. 1:18).
- The Spirit demonstrated the Father's approval of Jesus (Matt. 3:16–17).
- The Spirit empowered Jesus to cast out demons (Matt. 12:28).
- The Spirit guided and sustained Jesus (Luke 4:1, 14).
- Jesus testified to the Spirit's anointing on His life and ministry (Luke 4:16–21).

- The Spirit empowered Jesus for miracles and good works (Acts 10:37–38).
- The Spirit empowered Jesus to die on the cross (Heb. 9:14).
- And the Spirit raised Jesus from the dead (Rom. 8:11).

The Spirit is intimately involved with the work of Jesus, and everything the Spirit does points glory back to the Son. But when Jesus was on earth, since His actions were unprecedented, some people attributed them to demons (Matt. 12:27). In fact, many theologians believe this dismissal—rejection of the Spirit's work through Christ, accusing the Son of God of doing the works of the devil instead of the Spirit's work—is what Matthew 12:31 refers to as blasphemy of the Holy Spirit, or the "unforgivable/unpardonable sin."[4] Jesus's words and works were all Father-initiated and Spirit-empowered; a rejection of the Spirit is a rejection of the entire Trinity.

The Spirit never points to Himself in His work. He points to Jesus. Just look at how the Gospel of John makes this clear:

- He is sent by the Father, teaches us, and reminds us of Jesus's words (John 14:26).
- He's the Spirit of truth, He proceeds from the Father, and He bears witness about Jesus (John 15:26).
- He glorifies Jesus and declares the truths of Jesus (John 16:14).

If you've ever wondered what a Spirit-filled church or person looks like, look for the gospel of Jesus to be proclaimed—that's the pattern of how the Spirit works in Scripture. In Scripture, He never draws attention to Himself for the sake of awe or His own glory; His work is always a means to an end, and that end is the gospel of Jesus. The Spirit reveals Christ. In fact, when Jesus performed Spirit-empowered miracles and people were drawn to Him only for the miraculous performance and not His message, Jesus rebuked them (John 6:26). The Spirit isn't aiming merely to demonstrate God's power but to use that power to point to God!

Where the message of Jesus is being proclaimed, the Spirit is at work! In fact, one of the ways we most clearly see the Spirit at work is in the very existence of Scripture, which points us to Jesus. According to Jesus, Luke, Paul, and Peter, the Spirit authored Scripture through the hands of men (Matt. 22:43; Acts 1:16; 2 Tim. 3:16–17; 2 Pet. 1:21). He's the One who empowered and guided them as they wrote. Jesus said all Scripture points to Him (John 5:39–46), which is consistent with the rest of the Spirit's work. The Spirit uses His power to communicate the story of God's redemption and love through the work of Christ. This doesn't suggest that the Spirit is some kind of second-tier God. Instead, it reiterates what we've already established: the Persons of the Trinity aren't self-focused; they point to one another and are outgoing in their nature.

The Spirit in Relationship with Believers

The Spirit has been intimately involved with humans ever since His role in creating humanity (Ps. 104:30). When we see Him in the Old Testament, He is most often described as being "on" or "with" a person, and His actions are more transient, moving from person to person to empower them for a specific task. For instance, He came upon Saul to empower him to be king and then left Saul and came upon David when it was time for David to advance to the throne (1 Sam. 10:6; 16:13–14). The Spirit's presence indicated a specific anointing and appointing.

However, in the New Testament, the Father and Son sent the Spirit to indwell believers—to seal us and serve as the down payment (guarantee) on our kingdom inheritance. The Spirit is the means by which God is with us always (Matt. 28:20). This could be the primary reason Jesus said it was to our advantage for Him to leave and send His Spirit instead (John 16:7). The Spirit can be in all believers simultaneously and always—and He is! That is an incredible advantage!

All of the Spirit's actions and interactions on earth point us back to the relational beauty of the Trinity. Nothing He does is intended to put the spotlight on Himself. As we look at His work in our hearts, minds, and lives, we'll see that every aspect of the Christian life is empowered by the Spirit. There's no aspect of our relationship with God that is untouched by the Spirit, and no part of the time line when He isn't present and active: (a) God was already at work in our lives through

His Spirit to convict us of sin and draw us to Himself prior to our salvation; (b) He is the sign of our adoption and salvation; and (c) He remains at work in our lives continually as a result of our salvation.

Prior to Our Salvation

In the Old Testament, the Father gave the promise of a new heart and a new spirit (i.e., His Spirit) to His people (Ezek. 36:26–27). The Spirit revealed our need for salvation by convicting us of our sin and our need for a Savior when we were lost (John 16:7–11).

Jesus told His followers that the world would hate them, but He would send the Spirit to help them and counsel them (John 15:18–27). At the time He spoke this to them, the Spirit didn't yet permanently dwell in believers. Prior to this, the Spirit could come and go at any time, but Jesus knew that was all about to change. He was referencing a time when the Spirit would come to dwell within believers and never leave them.

In addition to serving believers in such beautiful ways (which we'll get to in a moment), the Spirit also serves those who don't know the Father. Just as He convicted us of our sins prior to our own salvation, He does this by convicting them of their sins. It's hard to view conviction of sin as being a gift or a blessing, but it is. Imagine if you were left to wander off in your sin, destroying everything you touched, but you didn't feel an ounce of guilt. Is that the kind of life you want? Wouldn't you want to be aware when you're hurting the people who love you and the people you love? Out of God's great patience and kindness, His Spirit convicts sinners and prompts them to repent. Romans 2:4 says His kindness leads us to repent. We were all born as sinners, created as a part of fallen humanity, and we will continue on that path unless God's Spirit calls us to repent. Here's how Jesus puts it in John 16:8–11:

> When he comes, he will convict the world concerning sin and righteousness and judgment: concerning sin, because they do not believe in me; concerning righteousness, because I go to the Father, and you will see me no longer; concerning judgment, because the ruler of this world is judged.

In the first part of this passage, we see that the Spirit convicts the world of its sin and judgment, but as we keep reading, we see that He also convicts—or convinces—believers of their righteousness. He reminds us who we really are. When sin calls our name, the Spirit of God reminds us of our identity as God's kids! Darkness isn't fitting for the children of light. He has called us into the light and shows us how to live in it. In a dark and broken world, God the Spirit guides us into truth and righteousness. Which brings us to His role in our salvation, where we first entered into such light and righteousness.

In Our Salvation

The Spirit makes us new and gives us eternal life (John 3:3–8; Rom. 8:10–11). He washes, regenerates, and renews us (Titus 3:5). He serves as the line of demarcation between the person who knows God and the one who doesn't—without Him, we don't belong to God (Rom. 8:9). He dwells in believers (1 Cor. 6:19). He is the marker of our adoption into God's family (Rom. 8:15), and He makes it possible for us to call God our Father (Gal. 4:6). Without His presence in us through salvation, we would merely be God's creation, not God's children. He is the seal of our salvation, forever marking us as God's possession (Eph. 1:13–14).

And salvation is not just God descending to humanity to rescue us from death and bring us joy in this life. Another beautiful result of our salvation is that, through the power of the Spirit, we're able to ascend with Christ and participate in the Trinity's eternal life and communion (Eph. 2:4–6; 1 John 1:1–4). There is a deep embedding where God unites us with Himself to receive His love eternally.

As a Result of Our Salvation

After we are adopted into God's family, the Spirit bears witness that we are God's children (Rom. 8:16). His work in the life of a believer is ongoing, fulfilling God's promise to finish what He started in us (Phil. 1:6). Without His power in our lives, we would be helpless, hopeless, and joyless! The

Spirit is sanctifying us, maturing us as believers, and continually shaping us to look more like Jesus (Rom. 8:29; 2 Cor. 3:18). He also provides guidance and direction for us as we seek to obey God (John 16:13; Rom. 8:26–27).

Ultimately, He moves us toward a fuller experience of true joy, hope, love, righteousness, and peace. Romans 5:5 says, "God's love has been poured into our hearts through the Holy Spirit who has been given to us." Romans 15:13 says, "May the God of hope fill you with all joy and peace in believing, so that by the power of the Holy Spirit you may abound in hope." And Romans 14:17 says, "The kingdom of God is not a matter of eating and drinking but of righteousness and peace and joy in the Holy Spirit."

Throughout the New Testament, Paul commands the church to keep the whole body of Christ in mind, to consider others, to walk in humility, and to serve others, just as Jesus did. It sounds like a complete overhaul of sinful humanity, right? But Paul was confident that God would finish what He started in them. He repeated this idea a few times in his letter to the Philippians. In 2:12–13, he said, "Work out your own salvation with fear and trembling, for it is God who works in you, both to will and to work for His good pleasure." He indicated that God is the one doing good works through them, and even creating the desire in them to do those things—to will and to work, for His good pleasure.

Here's one important point of clarification: Paul's encouragement to "work out their own salvation" was not a call to figure out how to save themselves. If we could do that, we wouldn't need a Savior or the Spirit. The context here, as well as in everything else Paul wrote, helps clarify that he was talking about living lives that demonstrate the gratitude and awe we feel toward God for saving us. This was a nod to the process of sanctification—where, as we've mentioned before, God works in us through His Spirit to conform us to the image of His Son.

The Spirit's activity in our lives is often subtle, specifically when it comes to areas like gaining a new understanding of spiritual truths or being encouraged in our faith. It's tempting to gloss over those things as normal everyday occurrences, but Scripture attributes those actions to the Spirit's loving work in our lives. Likewise, it can be easy to get puffed up about our obedience, as though we made ourselves live more righteously, but Scripture says the Spirit is the one who transforms us. Our obedience to God is His work in us.

Guarantee

We learn a lot about the Spirit's work in a letter the apostle Paul wrote to the church in Ephesus. When he was talking about Jesus, he said this in Ephesians 1:13–14: "In him you also, when you heard the word of truth, the gospel of your salvation, and believed in him, were sealed with the promised Holy Spirit, who is the guarantee of our inheritance until we acquire possession of it, to the praise of his glory." These two short verses hold rich theology, revealing a few unique things about the Spirit's roles in our lives.

First, He is the "guarantee"—or the deposit—of our inheritance in the kingdom of God. It's like when you put a down payment on a car or a house, signaling that you're buying it in full. God deposits His Spirit into us to show that He owns us and to confirm that He'll give us an inheritance as His kids.

Second, if we take Ephesians 1:13–14 along with Romans 8:9, which says that anyone who doesn't have the Spirit doesn't belong to God, we also see that the Spirit's indwelling presence is what differentiates between those who are God's kids and those who aren't. We receive the Holy Spirit the moment we believe and submit to the truth about who God is and the rescue He has provided for us through Jesus. The Spirit's presence in our lives serves as evidence that we have passed from death into eternal life.

And finally, we see that God has sealed us with the Spirit. In other words, one of the benefits of the Spirit being *in us* is that His presence *seals us* for all eternity. This particular type of seal refers to the way biblical kings—and really, kings throughout much of history—would press their signet ring into melted wax to mark their possessions and to secure any documents and letters sent with their authority.[5] The seal is a sign of ownership, and it's also a guarantee of security. When God puts His Spirit in us, we are marked as God's people forever. He's not going anywhere!

And while He's in us, He's not just taking it easy, kicking back in the hammock of our hearts. He is at work. In the sections below, we cover three ways the Spirit works in us—Sanctifier, Comforter, and Guide.

Sanctifier

First Corinthians 6:11 makes the Spirit's role clear when it comes to our sanctification: "You were washed, you were sanctified, you were justified in the name of the Lord Jesus Christ and by the Spirit of our God." But what does *sanctification* mean? It is the ongoing process of becoming more like Jesus over time—a process the Spirit of God increasingly works out in our hearts and minds from one degree to another as we walk through this life. Or, as Paul would put it in 2 Corinthians 3:18 (csb): "We all, with unveiled faces, are looking as in a mirror at the glory of the Lord and are being transformed into the same image from glory to glory; this is from the Lord who is the Spirit."

One way the Spirit helps us become more like Jesus over time is by bearing spiritual "fruit" in us (or Christian virtues)—the kind of fruit Jesus bore. The Bible calls this the fruit of the Spirit. Galatians 5:22–23 summarizes the Spirit's activity in the lives of believers by comparing it to fruit, but the word used in this passage is singular, not plural. It is one fruit with nine characteristics: love, joy, peace, patience, kindness, goodness, faithfulness, gentleness, and self-control. Those are the attributes of His fruit—one fruit, nine descriptions—just as you might find multiple ways to describe one apple.

The Spirit's fruit is the opposite of what our nature/flesh desires (Gal. 5:19–21), so while we live on this earth, we're being pulled in two directions. Said another way, the Spirit is at odds with the sinful desires we naturally experience (Eph. 5:18). But Paul encouraged us with these words, "Walk by the Spirit, and you will not gratify the desires of the flesh. For the desires of the flesh are against the Spirit, and the desires of the Spirit are against the flesh, for these are opposed to each other, to keep you from doing the things you want to do" (Gal. 5:16–17).

Paul told us to follow the Spirit's lead and then lovingly reminded us that we do this out of the joy of our relationship with God, not merely so we can keep God's law: "But if you are led by the Spirit, you are not under the law" (Gal. 5:18). Paul pointed out we're not self-righteous law abiders but Spirit-led fruit producers!

Spirit-fruit may grow slower than you want it to. Sometimes you may notice no progress, and the tree seems barren. In those times, we have to remind our hearts to rest on the finished work of Christ and trust in God's promise to complete what He started in us.

As the Spirit works in us to beautify, perfect, and sustain what the Father initiated and the Son fulfilled, have patience with yourself. Have you ever acted in a way that is contrary to your normal behavior? Not the kind of action you'd be embarrassed or ashamed of, but more along the lines of something beautiful you aren't used to seeing in yourself? Any time I've experienced that, it has always delighted me to see the Spirit at work in me.

For instance, I know how I typically respond to drivers who want to merge, who cut me off in traffic, or are driving too slow in the left lane. And it is not pretty. But in recent years I've seen verifiable evidence of the Spirit at work in my heart. Suddenly, my heart posture and my actions are different. I've gone from thinking, *Oh you want to merge? Not a chance! Maybe you should've planned ahead*, to thinking things like, *Oh you need help? I can help you! Come on over!*

I know myself, and that is not me. That's all Him. He's at work within me producing His Spirit fruit in my life: love, joy, peace, patience, kindness, goodness, faithfulness, gentleness, self-control. That's all Him.

Isn't it shocking? Isn't it delightful? I want more of that! I want more of the heart change He works in me. Again, this could be one of the primary reasons Jesus said it was better for His disciples if He went away and sent the Spirit instead— not only was the Spirit not limited to time and space like Jesus was during His time on earth, but He's also working on an internal level.

Our position as believers stands in stark contrast to those who don't know Christ. They don't have the Spirit or follow the Spirit, so they lean into the fruit of the flesh ("works of the flesh" in Gal. 5:19–21). Their lifestyle isn't all debauchery;

some of it looks more polished and admirable because it takes the shape of power and prestige or even self-focused morality.

In fact, Jesus regularly rebuked the Pharisees, a group of self-righteous leaders in Israel who worked hard to abide by the law. People who are bent on establishing their own righteousness refuse to submit to God (Rom. 10:1–4). Jesus said the world (as opposed to God's children) doesn't know the Spirit (John 14:16–17). And those who don't know God don't follow Him; they naturally rebel against Him.

As believers, we're less likely to reject God's work than an unbeliever, but we have another problem to face. If we don't know the details of who the triune God is and how He works in our lives, we're in danger of trying to do His work for Him. We're never told to imitate the Spirit. In fact, we're more frequently called to yield to the Spirit's power than to demonstrate it. We aren't told to be conformed to the Spirit; we're told to be conformed to Christ. The Spirit is the One who enables us to imitate Christ and gives us the desire to do so. His work in our lives is transformative in its nature. We cannot know Him without being moved toward righteousness, peace, and joy.

God the Spirit is our divine source of power and direction, but if we're captivated by that power because we want to use it for our own self-gratification and self-glorification, we not only miss the point, but we reveal our idolatry. The Spirit is for us but He is God. We are His servants, not vice versa.

Comforter

In a few translations of John 14:26, we see that Jesus referred to the Spirit as our "Comforter." Some of the many ways He comforts and helps us are by guiding us into truth (see the section below), by reminding us of our identity as God's adopted children, and by reminding us of our righteousness when we feel shame. He convinces us—convicts us—of our right standing with God (John 16:18)! Don't you need to be comforted with the truth the most when life is hard—whether as a result of your sin, the sins of others, or the circumstances of broken humanity? Isn't that when you most need to be reminded that God is your Father, that you are His child, and that He loves you in that very moment? And that's exactly what you get with God's Spirit, for "the Spirit himself testifies together with our spirit that we are God's children" (Rom. 8:16). When we are in challenging times, we're in the greatest space to see God's glory all the more, to see who He truly is. You are the recipient of the greatest gift any of us could ever receive—the Spirit of God, living in you!

Guide

Jesus also tells us that the Spirit is our helper and our guide (John 14:26; 16:13). He provides guidance for all the daily decisions we have to make, and it's vital that we seek Him.

A few years ago, I was trying to make a decision, and I consulted my mentor. The advice he gave me in that moment has served me well in a variety of other scenarios. He said, "Whatever you do, just don't light your own fires." I didn't understand his metaphor until he quoted Isaiah 50:10–11.

These two verses talk about two different types of people. Verse 10 says, "Who among you fears the Lord and obeys the voice of his servant? Let him who walks in darkness and has no light trust in the name of the Lord and rely on his God." It describes the man who trusts God. Even in the darkness, he knows he's not alone, and he leans into God, knowing He's with him.

Verse 11 describes a different kind of man. "Behold, all you who kindle a fire, who equip yourselves with burning torches! Walk by the light of your fire, and by the torches that you have kindled! This you have from my hand: you shall lie down in torment." The man in verse 11 trusts in his own ideas. He's driven by his own fears and struggles. He refuses to wait for God's guidance. He impatiently grapples for matches or lighters or pieces of flint—anything to escape the darkness of the moment.

Isaiah said this kind of man may find comfort in his makeshift torches, but that's the only comfort he'll know. In fact, he'll lie down in torment. The man-made torches will be such a fleeting comfort. He'll never know the beauty and joy and peace of trusting God in the dark and waiting for Him to bring the light.

The world may be telling you, "Follow your heart!," and your brain may be saying, "I think I can figure this out logically," but Proverbs 3:5–6 says, "Trust in the LORD with all your heart" (not put your trust in your own heart) and "lean not on your own understanding" (that means you don't solely rely on your own logic either). Instead, "in all your ways acknowledge Him, and He shall direct your paths" (NKJV). When we stop and acknowledge God in our decisions and ask Him to direct our steps, He does it through the guidance and prompting of His Spirit.

Sometimes He does it even when we don't ask. He intercedes when we don't know what to ask for (Rom. 8:26–27). He gives us understanding and wisdom (1 Cor. 2:12–13). He brings revelation, knowledge, enlightenment, hope, and power (Eph. 1:17–20). And He directs our steps (Acts 8:29).

Discerning the guiding voice of God can sometimes feel like one of the more challenging, nuanced aspects of walking with Him. Here's how I like to think about it: this is a relationship. And like any relationship, time spent together fosters increasing familiarity. The more time I spend in God's Word, the more I begin to recognize His character, the more I become familiar with the kinds of things He says and does (which usually comes in the form of a prompting that goes against my flesh's way of handling something). That's what it's like to get to know His voice.

If you and I met once, I probably wouldn't recognize your voice at a later date. But if my mom calls me from a blocked number and there's a bad connection, I can still recognize her voice even through the static. There are similarities between this and the communication we have in our relationship with God, but it will often (or always) require a bit of faith as we lean into obeying His voice.

The Spirit in Relationship with the Church

One of the most beautiful aspects of the church is the way the Spirit meets the needs of believers. If a church and its members are walking by the Spirit, they'll be leaning into the needs of their people. And because the body of Christ will always have needs and the Spirit knows what they need, He empowers believers in the church with gifts that will help meet those needs. He's so efficient!

"To each is given the manifestation of the Spirit for the common good" (1 Cor. 12:7). According to this verse (which was written to believers), God's Spirit dwells in you and manifests Himself through you as you serve the church. One way to see the Spirit at work in your life is to get involved in the ministries of your church. The gifts He gives for serving the church are wide and varied, but they always point us beyond ourselves to the common good. We don't serve for our own glory or self-esteem. We serve to advance His mission, and He gifts us accordingly.

The New Testament lists a sampling of the Spirit's gifts; but even in the Old Testament, we can see specific stories of individual people God, by His Spirit, equipped and empowered for the greater role of serving His people. Just look at the example of how He empowered a man named Bezalel to build a place for God to dwell:

> The LORD said to Moses, "See, I have called by name Bezalel the son of Uri, son of Hur, of the tribe of Judah, and I have filled him with **the Spirit of God**, with ability and intelligence, with knowledge and all craftsmanship, to devise artistic designs, to work in gold, silver, and bronze, in cutting stones for setting, and in carving wood, to work in every craft." (Exod. 31:1–5, emphasis added)

Or consider a man named Othniel whom God equipped in Judges 3:9–10 to judge, to go to war, and to defeat the enemy in order to serve the people of Israel:

> But when the people of Israel cried out to the LORD, the LORD raised up a deliverer for the people of Israel, who saved them, Othniel the son of Kenaz, Caleb's younger brother. **The Spirit of the LORD** was upon him, and he judged Israel. He went out to war, and the LORD gave Cushan-rishathaim king of Mesopotamia into his hand. And his hand prevailed over Cushan-rishathaim. (emphasis added)

As a final example, see how God, by His Spirit, granted David the type of leadership that impacted and blessed a whole nation in 2 Samuel 23:2:

> "The **Spirit of the Lord** speaks by me; his word is on my tongue." (emphasis added)

From Old Testament to New, the Spirit's giftings to us aren't about us; they are intended to serve those around us!

Spiritual gifts aren't personality adjacent. They're given by the Spirit and only show up when you have the Spirit. Since He participated in your creation (Job 33:4), He can be credited with your natural giftings too—your talents or abilities, like the way you're athletically inclined, good at math, or are a "born leader." But unlike your natural giftings or inclinations, your spiritual gift may be something you aren't naturally inclined toward. Both types of gifting are God-given and God-driven and are intended to serve others and point glory back to God.

For instance, when God called Moses to be a leader and a prophet in Exodus 4:10–17, Moses protested because he said he was not a gifted speaker. God reassured Moses, reminding him that He would give him all the necessary words. But God also generously provided him with a ministry partner who was naturally gifted at speaking, his brother Aaron. Even though Moses and Aaron existed before the indwelling of the Spirit, God has always been working in His people to fulfill His plan. God uses both our spiritual gifts and our natural gifts to accomplish His purposes. God knows what His people need, and He knows what our leaders need, and either through natural giftings or spiritual giftings, He meets those needs!

Scripture addresses and lists spiritual gifts multiple times: Romans 12:6–8; 1 Corinthians 12; Ephesians 4:11–16; and 1 Peter 4:10–11. What's interesting is that these lists include some repeat roles, but they don't fully overlap, which seems to indicate none of the lists is exhaustive. Since the gifts are different in every place Scripture mentions them, it seems to me that these lists are meant to adapt. The places where Scripture lists various spiritual gifts are in letters to churches or pastors of churches, and the lists all vary. Since the authors of Scripture were writing at the prompting of the Holy Spirit Himself, and since they felt compelled by the Spirit to adjust their lists, it gives us reason to believe that perhaps these lists can expand to meet the needs that happen to show up in each individual church. It is possible that more gifts will continue to be added as the needs of the church shift and change because God will continue to equip His people with the spiritual gifts required to meet those needs.

That's one reason I believe your spiritual gifts may change over the course of your life. There's a good chance your church may need different things at different times, and God will equip specific members with what they need in order to meet the needs of other members. This humbles us and blesses us all at once. It reminds us that we never stop needing each other!

Since you and I are called to be part of the church, then we are also the means by which God works in the church. Here's a simple analogy: if you work inside a grocery store, and that grocery store is in your neighborhood, then you're at work in your neighborhood. Likewise, if the Spirit is at work in us and we are in the church, then the Spirit is at work in the church. He's not just floating around writing sermons and parking cars and cleaning toilets without any humans involved. He does His work through us, and He gifts and equips us to do the work He is doing through us.

Scripture gives several examples of what the Spirit's work looks like in the church. It may surprise you that this doesn't always mean teaching or leading worship or giving biblical counsel. Sometimes the needs of the people in the church aren't related to the obvious forms of "ministry" on a Sunday morning, but because of how the Spirit works, He equips people with the gifts to meet those needs no matter when they arise, and suddenly those gifts function as a form of ministry and worship!

For instance, is there an elderly person in your church whose house is falling apart, who can't mow her own lawn anymore? Then the people in the church who step in to change her air filters and rake her leaves are demonstrating their spiritual gifts of mercy. Sure, that moment doesn't happen on a Sunday morning, and sure, you may not find "lawn mowing" in any of Scripture's lists of spiritual gifts, but it is absolutely a moment that a spiritual gift is being faithfully exercised!

This chapter may make you curious about your Spirit-given gifts. In my experience, the best and most helpful way to determine what spiritual gifts you have is to see how the church is being built up by your presence there. If you don't know, ask someone at your church! If he/she doesn't know, this may be a great time to look into volunteering or serving at your church. First Corinthians 12:11 says, "All these are empowered by one and the same Spirit, who apportions to each one individually as he wills." The word *wills* suggests this is a volitional act on His part. He is intentional about how He is using you to serve His kingdom! You and your role are not an accident or an oversight!

Paul also says we can ask God to give us spiritual gifts we don't have (1 Cor. 12:31; 14:1). Since they're given by God, the Giver is the one who chooses what to give. However, not having a certain gift doesn't excuse us from walking in obedience. For instance, we're all called to evangelize and share the gospel, even if we don't have the gift of evangelism. Those who have the gift may come off as a "natural" when it comes to sharing their faith with nonbelievers, but it doesn't mean the rest of us get a pass. The same goes for hospitality, mercy, and so on. Some are especially gifted at those things, but every disciple, no matter their giftings, is called to walk like Jesus in their daily life. Remember, our job is to focus simply on being faithful; by the power and presence of His Spirit, He's the one who brings the fruit!

In addition to His work in the believers within the church, the Spirit equips and guides the church by setting apart elders and ministers to lead it (Acts 13:2; 20:28). Ultimately, through all His acts within individual believers and the church at large, the Spirit drives us toward deeper joy. Acts 13:52 says, "The disciples were filled with joy and with the Holy Spirit." All of His giftings and comfort, all of His truth and help, all of His sanctifying power and His reminders of our eternally secure relationship—He's the One who makes all those things possible for us. He fills us with joy because He's where the joy is!

5

Prayer and Communication

Three Foundations of the Trinity

1. There is only one true God.

2. There are three divine Persons of the one true God.

3. The three Persons are co-equal,
co-eternal, and co-relational.

*"The only person who dares wake up a king
at 3:00 AM for a glass of water is a child. We
have that kind of access."* —Tim Keller[1]

Communication Basics

People have written many books on prayer, but our focus here will be less on learning how to pray and more on understanding how our view of the Trinity informs and directs our prayers. The way we communicate with the triune God is fully informed by how we view Him and how much we understand about His actions in our lives. Before we look at how we communicate with Him, let's recap what we've learned about the Trinity so far. It's foundational for every interaction with Him.

God the Father, Son, and Spirit are all intimately involved in the story of our redemption. In the past three chapters, we've looked at their unique roles as they apply to humanity (the **Economic Trinity**). It's important for us to remember that God's actions toward us are borne out of who He is (the **Immanent Trinity**). He isn't triune because He behaves in these ways; His triune nature precedes and informs all His triune actions.

Here's a brief overview, summarized from Ephesians 1:3–14.

The Father: Our creation, salvation, and restoration originated with the Father. He chose us before the foundation of the world and planned to adopt us as His children (Eph. 1:3–6). His plan was accomplished and applied through the other Persons of the Trinity.

The Son: He accomplished the work of our creation, salvation, and redemption. The Son is the means by which the Father does His saving work in our lives—including our forgiveness, reconciliation, justification, sanctification, and glorification (Eph. 1:7–12).

The Spirit: The Father's salvation (accomplished through the Son) is communicated to us by His Holy Spirit. God gives us His Spirit to dwell in us—making us new, granting us faith, changing us from the inside out, and continuing in us the sanctifying work of conforming us to the image of Christ. The Spirit establishes and confirms that we are God's children, and He serves as a guarantee of our salvation (Eph. 1:13–14).

Each Person of the Trinity played a unique role in our creation, salvation, and restoration. The Father authored our salvation; the Son accomplished it, and the Spirit applied it. Knowing that all of this goodness originated with the Father's plan (James 1:17) should endear our hearts to Him. It should serve as a reminder that we are welcomed at His throne and His table (Heb. 4:16). Scripture repeatedly reveals that the Father loves to hear from His children, and He wants us to talk to Him all the time. Not only that, but He also delights to give good gifts to His children (Matt. 7:11; Luke 12:32).

Consider how Tim Chester sums it up in his book *Delighting in the Trinity*:

> Some people look for security in a subjective experience of the Spirit; others in the objective work of Christ. But Christian assurance encompasses both for it has a threefold basis in trinitarian grace. It is rooted in the electing

love of the Father, the finished work of the
Son, and the present witness of the Spirit.[2]

Because all three Persons of the Trinity are involved in our
creation, salvation, and redemption, it should be no surprise
that all three Persons are involved in our prayer life too. In
Scripture, the normative way to pray is to the Father, through
the Son, by the Spirit. We'll cover that in greater depth later
in this chapter. The Father is the initiator of all good things,
and He's the one who initiates communication with us. Jesus
bridged the gap between us and the Father so that we could
speak to the Father directly, and His Spirit came to dwell in
us as well—which means we have a way to constantly communicate back and forth.

The more you read your Bible, the more the Spirit will
speak to you. Jesus said the Spirit will remind us of what He
has said (John 14:26). And you can't be *re*minded of something you were never *minded* of to begin with. The Holy Spirit
is the one who authored Scripture through the hands of men,
so the more you know what He says and the way He talks,
the easier it will be for you to recognize His voice when He
prompts you.

Especially if you're new to dedicated prayer and Bible reading, it may be challenging for you to separate your thoughts
from His. That's a common challenge. But the more you
know Scripture, the more you'll have a measuring stick to hold
those thoughts against to see where they line up and where
they don't. You won't always get it right, but that's okay. Keep

asking Him to help you and lead you into wisdom. He promised wisdom for all who ask (James 1:5). What an incredible gift! We all need it, He's got it all, and He shares!

In general, it may be helpful to think of prayer with the triune God as a simple conversation. You're talking to Someone. However, in this scenario, the Person listening is the God who already knows everything about you, loves you, and never grows tired of hearing from you. In fact, He encourages us to make prayer a continual part of our days (1 Thess. 5:16–18)—not just when we're in a challenging situation or when we're about to eat a meal but all throughout the day.

His Word tells us to "rejoice always, pray without ceasing, give thanks in all circumstances; for this is the will of God in Christ Jesus for you" (1 Thess. 5:16–17). There are very few places in Scripture where something is clearly stated as being "God's will for you," but this is one of those places. It's His will for you to always be in communication with Him! And of course, the more we learn about who He is, the more we can easily incorporate rejoicing and thankfulness into those times of communication with Him.

It also may be helpful to remember that prayer can be taught and learned—it's a conversational skill you can improve on over time. After overhearing Jesus's prayers to the Father, the disciples asked Him to teach them how to pray (Luke 11:1–13), and He gave them a model to use when they talked to the Father.

Several acrostics can help us integrate the specifics Jesus taught. My current favorite is the PRAY method: Praise, Repent, Ask, Yield. There's also the ACTS method: Adoration, Confession, Thanksgiving, Supplication. Whatever helpful form you use or don't use, your prayer life can thrive as a result of your growing knowledge of the Trinity, as you implement the truths of whom you're addressing and how.

Perhaps you're one of the people who often address your prayers to "Jesus." Maybe praying to "God" just feels too generic, and you want the people overhearing you to know which God you're praying to—the God of Christianity. Or maybe it's hard to pray to the Father because you've had a strained relationship with your earthly dad, and it's challenging to stomach the idea of calling God by that same name.

The line of thought is certainly understandable because **at its heart, prayer is a relational endeavor**. It's communication. But God is not your earthly father. He's *the* Father. The way we communicate with the triune God is fully informed by the way we view Him and how much we understand about His actions in our lives. We don't communicate well with people we misunderstand or don't trust.

For instance, if you didn't believe God was powerful, you wouldn't ask Him to do big things. If you didn't believe He was attentive and caring, you wouldn't ask Him to do small things. If you didn't believe He was loving and merciful, you wouldn't confess your sins because you'd fear His punishment. But the more you know God's character, the more you can talk to Him rightly, the more you'll approach Him with the right perspective.

Praying Out of Fear?

One frequently misunderstood aspect of how we relate to God and His character comes from Scripture's repeated command to fear Him. It took me a long time to understand what that phrase meant.

In Scripture there are two kinds of fear: the first is the kind we're most familiar with—it's a terror, of sorts. That kind of fear usually relates to destruction, and since we fear destruction, we run. For instance, if you're afraid of spiders, you may scream when you see one or cover your eyes when they come on the screen. Or if you saw a bear in the woods, your natural instinct would be to run as fast as you can away from it. That's the "terror" type of fear.

The other kind of fear is exclusively used in Scripture to point to the fear of the Lord. It does not make us want to run. In fact, it's used in ways that portray Him as lovely and inviting. It draws us in instead of pushing us away. While we'd usually avoid praying out of fear in the "terror" sense of the word, the Bible reveals that we actually *should* pray out of a *godly* fear of the Lord! This concept is foundational to our understanding of God and prayer, so let's take some time to explore this idea as it shows up in Scripture:

- Consider Psalm 130:4 which says: "With You, there is forgiveness, that You may be feared." **The fear of God consists primarily of delight and awe.** If that weren't true, the two halves of this verse wouldn't fit together at all. It would have to say, "With You there is punishment, that You may be feared." Instead, this verse reminds us that God's great forgiveness of our sins inspires a deeper level of respect and awe and delight. It draws us to Him. Regardless of what kinds of iniquity and rebellion you've given in to, you can come to Him for forgiveness, knowing that Christ has fully paid for your sins, and you have pardon, redemption, and righteousness because of Him.

- Next, read Luke 7:16. It is talking about the response of the locals after Jesus raised a young man from the dead. It says, "**Fear seized them all, and they glorified God**, saying, 'A great prophet has arisen among us!' and 'God has visited his people!'" (emphasis added). Fear seized them and caused them to glorify God? They praised Him? When I'm afraid in the "terrified" sense, I don't praise; I run. But when Jesus

came on the scene and demonstrated His
healing power, they were awe inspired.
That's what the fear of the Lord looks
like. Delight and awe. It results in praising
and glorifying Him!

- Psalm 112:1 says, "Praise the LORD!
  Blessed is the man who fears the LORD,
  who greatly delights in his commandments!" (emphasis added). Blessed is the
  man who fears the Lord? In Scripture,
  the word "blessed" can also be translated
  as "happy." If this were the terrified kind
  of fear, it wouldn't coexist with happiness,
  but this verse says fear of the Lord is adjacent to delight.

- This next verse shows us both kinds of fear
  in the same verse, and it even juxtaposes
  them so we can see the contrast. Exodus
  20:20 covers the events right after God
  gave His people the Ten Commandments.
  Moses told the people, **"Do not fear,"**—
  the bad kind, the terrified kind—"for
  God has come to test you, that the **fear
  of him**"—the good kind, the enticing
  kind—"may be before you, that you may
  not sin" (emphasis added). Again, regular
  fear is what makes us want to run away

from something, but the fear of the Lord invites us into the kind of intimacy with Him that produces righteousness in us!

- Psalm 147:11 says, "**The LORD takes pleasure in those who fear him,** in those who hope in his steadfast love" (emphasis added). How incredible! Those who fear the Lord are those who hope in His love. And He takes pleasure in them!

- In Jeremiah 32:40–41, God says, "I will make with them an everlasting covenant, that I will not turn away from doing good to them. And **I will put the fear of me in their hearts,** that they may not turn from me. I will rejoice in doing them good, and I will plant them in this land in faithfulness, with all my heart and all my soul" (emphasis added). God is the one who puts this good kind of fear in our hearts— this delight and awe. He helps us delight in Him. He keeps us near Him. He prompts us to obey. He rejoices in doing us good!

Godly and biblical fear of the Lord enhances our lives in every way! **To fear God is to see Him rightly—in all of His beauty and power and wisdom and goodness.** In its purest sense, fearing God means giving Him the greatest weight or value in your life. To be clear: our delight in Him doesn't make us forget that He has supreme power over everything in the universe; it just makes that power awe inspiring instead of terrifying. It's a *good* kind of fear. So yes, pray in fear to God—the right kind of fear!

Allow me to borrow a friend's comparison to something in the natural realm. He says the good fear is kind of like how we feel about the Grand Canyon—we're so drawn to it that we plan entire trips around it, and we drive for hours to reach the site where we look over the edge and stand in awe of its beauty and depth—but all the while, we're fully aware that it could kill us.

It's important to grasp this concept as part of our prayer overview because **we won't pray rightly to a God we fear wrongly.** We have to have the right kind of fear, the delight-and-awe kind of fear. The kind of fear that draws us in is exclusively used in Scripture to point to the fear of the Lord.

How God Communicates with Us

In your relationship with God, He is the initiator. It only takes a quick glance at these passages below to see this truth on full display:

- "We love because he first loved us" (1 John 4:19). You didn't love God first. He loved you first!
- "No one can come to me unless the Father who sent me draws him" (John 6:44). You

didn't draw yourself to the Father. The
Father drew you to Himself!

- "No one can come to me unless it is
  granted him by the Father" (John 6:65).
  God grants you the ability to come to
  Him, not the other way around.
- "Behold, I stand at the door and knock. If
  anyone hears my voice and opens the door,
  I will come in to him and eat with him,
  and he with me" (Rev. 3:20). *The Lord* is
  the one who pursues a deeper relationship
  and conversation with you.

The Father initiates communication with us, His people,
because He longs to be united with us. But our sin nature
means we're separated from Him, which inhibits our communication. But praise God—He had a plan for this all along!
Not only did Jesus bridge the gap by granting us His righteousness and making a way for us to approach the Father,
but the Spirit came to dwell in us as well, giving us access to a
constant flow of communication with God. Just as the Father,
Son, and Spirit work together for our creation, salvation, and
redemption, they also work together toward our conversation.
The Father takes action through the Son by the Spirit, and
that's the shape of our communication with Him as well.

Jesus promised us that the Spirit would remind us of
His words (John 14:26). God communicates with us via His
Spirit, who equips us with the mental and spiritual truth that

Jesus taught and lived and is. As the Spirit works in us, He equips us to think like Jesus thought and live out of the same truth. He can, quite literally, change our minds. This is beautiful, paradigm-shifting news for you if you've ever felt drawn to something you knew wouldn't benefit you or if you've lacked a love for the things of God. If you, like Paul, have ever felt trapped by your own heart and sin patterns (Rom. 7:13–25), the Spirit gives you hope for better things—the mind of Christ (Phil. 2:5)! He communicates the truth to us in the midst of sin's lies!

In addition to speaking truth to us through Scripture and the Spirit, God helps us in other ways. Jesus makes intercession for us (Rom. 8:34; Heb. 7:25), and the Spirit helps us in our weakness and prays for us according to God's will when we don't know what to say (Rom. 8:26–27).

Both the Son and the Spirit are praying for you. Not only is this a great comfort, but it's a great promise. God didn't save you then abandon you. He is praying for you. According to 1 Corinthians 2:10–11, the Spirit knows the thoughts of the Father, and, in fact, they share a will and nature, so the Spirit is praying things for you that align with the Father's heart and His plan for you. God has promised to always answer yes to prayers that align with His will (1 John 5:14–15), which means these prayers prayed by God to God are ones He will answer with a yes. None of them are fruitless or frivolous. They all point toward your redemption and your ultimate joy!

Not only does the Spirit pray to the Father on our behalf, but He also teaches us how to pray to the Father (1 Cor. 2:10–11). If you've ever felt like you're not good at praying or you feel awkward praying in front of others, take heart! The Spirit is willing and able to teach you how to pray. We can learn from Him through the examples of prayer He has shown us in Scripture, including when Jesus taught His disciples how to pray. As the Spirit teaches us, He also serves as a conduit for our communication with the Father. He never angles for our attention; He's always pointing us back to the Father through the work of the Son.

There may be other ways we sense God relaying His attributes or His plans to us—through His creation, music, circumstances, or through others. We'll talk more about that last option in the final chapter.

How We Communicate with God

The structure of trinitarian prayer mirrors both the way God communicates with us and imparts salvation to us. The Father communicates with us through the connection established by the work of His Son, sustained by the power of the Spirit. And our responsive prayer to Him flows through that same process of communication: we pray by the Spirit, through the Son, to the Father.

Typically, **we pray to the Father.** In the Lord's Prayer, Jesus instructed His followers to pray to the Father (Matt. 6:9–13).

That doesn't mean we can't or shouldn't pray to the Son or Spirit, but it shows us that the normative way of praying is directed to the Father. Jesus tells us that the Father is a willing listener who is eager to give good gifts to His children. As Sam Allberry says, "The God who had the idea of you is interested in you. . . . He is a God far more willing to answer and hear our prayers than we are to offer them."[3]

We pray to the Father through the Son. Jesus is the One who bridges the gap between us and the Father—that's what it means to pray "in His name." It's not a magical add-on that ensures we get what we ask for; it's the key for entry into the conversation. He is always the mediator for our conversations with the Father. Praying in His name is a reminder that we don't come on our own merit or performance but on His merit and performance. It's an invitation to always show up in prayer because we can be certain the Father's desire to hear us is unchanging, unyielding.

Because Jesus bridged the gap, we can approach the throne of grace with confidence, knowing God will hear us and will show us mercy and help us when we need it (Heb. 4:16). No matter what sin you've committed, no matter how much you've failed, you're welcome at His throne. Then, on the other hand, when you feel like you've nailed it as a Christian and pride creeps in, coming to the Father through the Son and in His name humbles us. We can't come to the Father in our own names. As Allberry says, "We come to the Father not by the sweat of our brow but by the blood of his Son."[4]

We pray to the Father through the Son, by the Spirit.
Allberry added, "No Christian prayer happens apart from the
work of the Spirit. We may not be mindful of that as we pray,
but it is true."[5] According to Romans 8, the effect of the Spirit
in our lives is that we're not only adopted into God's family,
but we also rightly recognize ourselves as God's children—we
gain a sense of our new, true identity. As we pray, we're deep-
ening and strengthening our relationship with God because
we're engaging with Him more and more. The Spirit comes
alongside us and helps us know how to pray.

Since He is with us, indwelling us as we pray, we never
pray alone. And none of our prayers are wasted, even if God's
answer to our prayer is no.

Many of us learned to pray by listening to others pray.
We may have learned patterns that feel formal or "right," but
some of them likely hold no meaning to us. If we've never
taken the time to understand prayer by studying the examples
in Scripture, it may feel like a meaningless exercise, like divine
small talk. Or it may seem like a chore. As C. S. Lewis says,
"Prayer is irksome. An excuse to omit it is never unwelcome.
. . . We are reluctant to begin," and yet, when we finally set-
tle into it, "we are delighted to finish."[6] There's a reason we
are delighted to finish: because prayer is so much more than
divine small talk or a chore!

Since prayer is communicating with the living God, let's
begin with what we know about Him. Let's not just oper-
ate out of habits that aren't informed by our relationship with

Him. Now that we know more about Him, we can talk to Him in ways that are more honest, accurate, and personal— and when we bend our prayer life around the truth of *who He truly is as Trinity*, our relationship with God will begin to take on richer textures and deeper joys! Or, as John Piper would put it, "The theological mind exists" not to simply acquire random factoids about God, but in our prayer and worship and every other spiritual endeavor, "to throw logs into the furnace of our affections for Christ."[7]

Topics

God invites us to talk to Him about all things, but we often find ourselves only lifting up a handful of categories to Him. Some people primarily pray to ask for personal help, while others pray only for others. Some spend most of their time in praise and gratitude, afraid to ask for anything, while others offer only confession or regret.

Most of the prayers we see throughout Scripture aren't aimed at personal success; they're oriented toward a personal knowing of God. But it's not just informational knowledge; it's relational knowledge. For those who truly seek God in prayer, the relationship is not only central; it is supreme. It is the most important goal, and that perspective is what drives the conversation.

When we pray, we're participating in the trinitarian life, engaging with all three Persons of the Trinity. If your prayers are self-seeking and you only talk to God in order to ask Him for what you want, consider this an invitation to talk to God about deeper things. The point of prayer is not to get what we want; the point of prayer is to get God. The more intimate a relationship is, the less we're able to function autonomously—we consider the other person, we look to honor him/her in our words and actions. And so it is with God. Through intimacy with Him, we connect with the source of all good things (John 15:5–11), and intimacy comes from the private conversation of prayer. How comforting it is to know that God wants prayer that is rooted in intimacy, not showiness. He doesn't care how many syllables your words have or how many words you use (Matt. 6:7–8)—He's after your heart!

Tone

To paraphrase Fred Sanders: in the New Testament, we get to eavesdrop on Jesus's prayers to the Father. We get to hear the things He told the disciples about the Spirit. We hear the Father's words to the Son. Lots of these things happen in public settings, and Jesus even prayed aloud, letting others hear and see the intimacy of His relationship with the Father. We get a glimpse into the unity of the Triune.[8] Gerald Bray said, "Christians have been admitted to the inner life of God."[9]

The prayers of Jesus also reveal His deep gratitude toward the Father (Luke 22:17–19; John 11:38–42) and a rejoicing in the Holy Spirit (Luke 10:21). One of the things we learn from eavesdropping on Jesus's prayers is that He thanks and praises the Father. He acknowledges the Father's role in things both big and small—from providing the food to His attention to Jesus's prayers to the way He works in the hearts of humanity. When we see how Jesus talks to the Father, we get a glimpse into the Father as our ultimate Provider, loving Father, and sovereign King.

Our hearts should arc toward God with gratitude and praise in all things. As we've already seen, the Bible calls us to "rejoice always, pray without ceasing, give thanks in all circumstances; for this is the will of God in Christ Jesus for you" (1 Thess. 5:16–18). The rejoicing and gratitude Jesus demonstrated is what God desires from us as well. While he was in prison, Paul told the church in Philippi to rejoice, to be reasonable, to be prayerful, and to be peaceful—he tied these things together in one stream of thought (Phil. 4:4–7). Rejoicing sets the tone—it bends our hearts toward God and His goodness. When that's our focus, we can move through life with reasonableness. When we're aware of the nearness of the Lord, we are quicker to remember that we don't have to strive after anything. He can be trusted to work on our behalf.

Asking in His Name

One of the more shocking statements Jesus made about prayer was when He told the disciples He would give them anything they asked in His name (John 15:7; 17:7). There are a few things worth pointing out from that conversation.

First, this seems to be in the context of walking out His power and doing these miraculous works. We can't just pull these verses out of their original context to make them mean whatever we want them to mean.

Second, He said these requests have to be made *in His name*, which ultimately means "in accordance with His will," because His name, personhood, and will are inseparable from one another. He's certainly not saying, "If you ask Me for a Maserati and end it with the phrase *'in Jesus's name, amen,'* then My hands are tied and I have to give you the Maserati!" In ancient times, a person's name was connected to their character and their will.[10] So essentially Jesus was saying, "Whatever you ask the Father that aligns with who I am and what I have planned, He will do it!" In other words, praying "in Jesus's name" has to do with aligning our hearts with His will. This is about surrendering to Him and honoring Him.

This may feel frustrating. You may wonder, *If God always gets His way, then why would we even bother to ask?* First, I find it helpful to remember that we *want* God to get His way. I'm familiar with my way, and it is often not good, to say the least. His way is always best because He can see beyond our current situation and into the ways a certain circumstance affects our future, our relationships, our character, our whole life. If we could see from that divine vantage point and factor in everything God is able to factor in (which we can't), we'd pray in line with it. As Tim Keller says, "You can come before God with the confidence that he is going to give what you would have asked for if you knew everything he knows."[11] Second, when God tells us to ask—and He does, repeatedly—He's inviting us into relationship. This is about conversation, about intimacy. Jesus wants our hearts to be so woven into His that all our desires start to take on His shape. Jesus said the Father is glorified in this—the Father wants us to bear the fruit of being united to Jesus!

Jesus said that if we abide in Him and His words abide in us, then we can ask whatever we want and He'll do it (John 15:7). This feels like a free pass, doesn't it? It sounds like we get everything we want. But even Jesus didn't get everything He wanted (Luke 22:42). In His humanity, He still had moments He experienced desire for an easier set of circumstances but ultimately submitted to the Father's will. And our humanity has to submit to the same! Which means we won't always get what we want just because we ask Him for it. The key idea here is directly related to our abiding in Him, being so united to Him that His word abides in us to the degree that when we ask for something, we will be asking in conjunction with His will. We will be asking for things He delights to say yes to, because our hearts will be aligned with His. This statement is about abiding, not acquiring.

Persistence

Jesus encouraged His followers to pray and not lose heart. In order to do that, we have to trust the Father's heart. Otherwise, why would we keep praying and talking to Him? Without knowing and trusting the Father's heart, it is easy for us to lose heart. Jesus knew it would be vital for His followers to understand that the Father was working on their behalf, even when they couldn't see it.

In Luke 18:1–8, Jesus told a parable about a needy widow and an unrighteous judge. A widow repeatedly goes to the judge to beg for justice against her adversary, and the judge finally relents because he's so annoyed by the woman's persistence. But make no mistake—the judge in this story is not like the Father. That's the whole point. Jesus described the judge as unrighteous, neither fearing God nor respecting man. So the point is this: if this wicked judge will actually work to grant justice to this woman, won't our loving heavenly Father do it all the more for His kids?

Jesus encourages His followers to keep talking to God about the things they desire because God's heart toward them is kind and He delights to give them good things (Matt. 7:11; Luke 12:32). Don't be a "one and done" type of believer when it comes to prayer. Keep going!

Worship

We tend to think of worship merely as the moment we sing songs to God in church. But as James B. Torrance put it: "Worship is . . . our participation through the Spirit in the Son's communion with the Father, in his vicarious life of worship and intercession."[12] Worship is being welcomed into and participating in the loving relationship the Father has with the Son. Romans 12:1 provides a helpful way of viewing worship as well; it teaches us that worship goes far beyond offering praise or songs to God, rather it is a *whole life* offered to God—and that includes prayer! This means we should view prayer as a form of worship, as it reminds us of how deeply embedded we are in the life and community of the triune God and arcs our hearts toward Him as we engage with Him in conversation.

In Scripture, prayer is compared to incense, praise, and sacrifice (Ps. 141:2; Rev. 5:8). God treasures and values our prayers. Prayer is one way we not only connect with Him but how we honor Him as well. Incense was a tool the ancient Jews used as part of their worship process in the temple. Not only are our prayers received as worship, but they're presented in treasured vessels, golden bowls. It's astonishing that God regards the prayers of His people so highly—to count them as worship, to cherish and guard them. Your prayers are valuable to God! He loves to communicate with you!

The Mysteries of Prayer

Prayer remains mysterious to us even as we engage in it. Sometimes we let that mystery intimidate us and keep us from communicating with the Father. Emilie Griffin astutely sums up our hesitation in this way:

> We may have built walls against prayer, against the presence of God, because of things he has not given us, things we thought we deserved. We may be blind to the blessings He has given us and think only of those things He

has withheld. We may be refusing to enter
into any mentality that accepts loss and defeat
as trials given for our growth and perfection.
We may be refusing to pray because we don't
intend for God to have it His way.[13]

But it doesn't have to be this way. As we're learning more
about trinitarian prayer, this is your opportunity to lean in—
don't let what you don't yet know stop you. In fact, the impulse
to pray comes to us from God Himself; He is relational, and
He communicates within Himself and with us!

Scripture encourages us with reminders that our God is
both attentive and generous. He invites us to ask and reminds
us that He is in the business of meeting all our needs (John
16:23–24; James 4:2).

Our God is eager to give! It's His nature. And He can
only give what is good and best. Even in the difficult things
that come our way, the eternal reality is that our Father can
be trusted. And our trust in Him can coexist with any pain,
sadness, or anger we may feel in our current circumstances.
He aches with us. Knowing that it's not in our good Father's
nature to give bad gifts, we can pray and ask while we ache
and wait.

It's challenging to understand why God might tell His
children "no" or "wait" when they ask for something. There
is no easy remedy for the pain this can bring to our relationship with Him. No single answer can explain His reasoning
because it is often beyond our understanding. Efforts to make

sense of His ways can ring hollow or lack compassion. Still, trusting Him in those dark times of denial and waiting can bring an intimacy with Him that comforts us—an intimacy we can't experience any other way.

Every time we come before God, humble ourselves in His presence, and ask Him to meet our needs, it shows we acknowledge Him as the source of all things. When we pray, we declare our faith in His character and His ways. But we must be careful to remember that this is our faith in Him, not faith in our faith or faith in our actions. I can't believe something hard enough to make it happen, and I can't force His hand through my obedience. He's not indebted to me, and He doesn't owe me a yes. It's easy to assume that if we want something and it's not sinful, then it is good, and we deserve it. But God's plan involves giving us more than just what we perceive as good—He's determined to give us what is best in the scope of eternity, and that's something we don't have the wisdom to perceive!

This is why we want God to say no to us at times. We can't even begin to conceive the things He has in store for us! Our plans are far too small and temporary. His plans to bless us exceed our ability to imagine. Surely you've begged God for something you later thanked Him for saying no to. I know I have! His no is always for the greatest good, and as we've noted before, because we aren't eternal like He is, we don't have eyes to see what He sees.

Though we've explored this earlier, it bears repeating: even Jesus, being fully God and fully man, had human longings that the Father said no to. In Luke 22:42, on the night before Jesus died, He prayed, "Father, if you are willing, remove this cup from me. Nevertheless, not my will, but yours, be done." And in knowing what the eternal plan was, Jesus's human nature submitted to the Father's will. Again, our humanity must do likewise.

How do we make sure we're yielded to God in prayer and that we're not trying to take over for Him? We need the Spirit's help. Paul told us that we should pray "at all times in the Spirit" (Eph. 6:18). What does that mean? When quoting Meyer's Commentary, John Piper described it like this: praying in the Spirit is praying in such a way so "that the Holy Spirit is the *moving* and *guiding* power" of the prayer.[14] In other words, we are actively engaging with Him as we pray, decidedly yielding to His guidance, not autonomously praying out of our own desires and experiences.

Draw near to Him in prayer today. He will meet you there—in your longings, confusion, sin, and gratitude—and He will be the loving Father you need in all those categories. He's where the joy is!

6

In His Image

Three Foundations of the Trinity

1. There is only one true God.
2. There are three divine Persons of the one true God.
3. The three Persons are co-equal,
co-eternal, and co-relational.

Now that we've seen how our understanding of the Trinity informs our primary relationship—the one we have with God—our final chapter will look at how our understanding the Trinity informs all our secondary relationships—with the world around us. None of the knowledge we're gaining terminates on us. God doesn't teach us things so we can feel smart and win arguments. This knowledge of Him equips us to love Him and others as His Spirit works in our hearts and lives.

Creation and Recreation

> Then God said, "Let us make man in our image, after our likeness." . . . So God created man in his own image, in the image of God He created him; male and female he created them. (Gen. 1:26–27)

The triune God not only worked together in unity and diversity to create us, but all three Persons of the Trinity also worked together in our *re*-creation (Ezek. 36:26–27). They were all active in both your natural birth and your spiritual birth (re-creation, salvation). God the Father caused you to be born again through the resurrection of Jesus Christ (1 Pet. 1:3), and God the Spirit serves as the guarantee of your salvation, conforming you to the image of Christ (2 Cor. 3:18; Rom. 8:29).

The position from which God created the world was one of love and glory. Many theologians believe this is what prompted Him to create the world—to share His infinite happiness and joy with us! What that ultimately means for us is that we will only find true happiness and joy as we connect with His identity and purpose—loving and glorifying God with a love that points us outside ourselves to Him and to others.

In fact, that is precisely how Jesus summarized all of the commands of God: love God, love others (Matt. 22:37–40). It's the very purpose for which we were created. Paul reminded us of this when He called us to "be imitators of God" (Eph. 5:1). If our created purpose is to love and connect with Him, then it stands to reason we would sense a compelling need to live toward that purpose. God generously created that need to point our hearts back to Himself so that we wouldn't be left to wander. Our hearts are prone to seek purpose and fulfillment in a million different temporary things, but He knows He's the true and eternal fulfillment of our needs.

Richard Sibbes put it so well: "If God had not a communicative, spreading goodness, he would never have created the world. The Father, Son, and Holy Ghost were happy in themselves, and enjoyed one another before the world was. Apart from the fact that God delights to communicate and spread his goodness, there had never been a creation or redemption."[1]

Conformed to Christ (Who Made the Father Known)

Adam and Eve were created in God's image, but did that all change when they sinned? Was His image in humanity ruined or lost? Not according to Scripture. Thank God, His image in us extends beyond the garden of Eden. It wasn't erased by the fall.

To summarize Donald Macleod in *Shared Life*, we retain the image of God for as long as we live, despite our sin.[2] That goes for even those who don't know God. Being made in God's image means we all have equal worth even in our diversity, and it means we're built for community and fellowship, just like the triune God. According to Genesis 9:6 and James 3:9, the way we treat others matters because people are made in God's image. He has given us—and others—an inherent dignity and value that sin doesn't erase. In fact, it provides more of an opportunity for God's nature and glory to be displayed.

While we were created in the image of God, and that image was broken and marred by the fall of man, God is still determined to have children who look like Him and display Him to the world. So He sets about conforming us to the image of His Son through the work of His Spirit. The triune God refuses to give up on His kids despite our brokenness.

The Purpose of the Fall

As we've discovered earlier in this book, the Father initiated our redemption story. It was His plan all along. He created the world from a position of love and glory, and it seems like His purpose was to share His infinite happiness and joy with us! The overarching story Scripture paints of the God who is outside of time is that this was always the plan. It wasn't a failed experiment. The fall of man and God's subsequent redemption of mankind was always plan A. I believe all Scripture teaches that all of this was planned, necessary, and beautiful. Let's look briefly at each of these.

First, I believe Scripture teaches it was planned. It didn't catch God off guard. Scripture reveals a God who is three things (of many): sovereign, omniscient, and outside of time. Even if He were only one of those things, it would be impossible for Him to be surprised by man's decision to rebel against Him, but the fact that He is all three sufficiently clarifies it. Revelation 13:8 says the Lamb was slain and our names were written in His book even before the foundation of the world! Think about this: if you're in Christ, before the world was even created, your name was written as one who would be redeemed from sin and granted life in God. Which means God knew the whole story before it ever played out. He's been in loving control of the whole thing from the start!

Second, I believe Scripture teaches it was necessary. If man had never fallen, but had lived as perfect and flawless, we wouldn't need to be redeemed. In the story of redemption, we're not the perfect, flawless heroes. God is. The story of redemption reveals the truth of the situation: we're not God, and He is the one worthy of being praised. Mankind was always destined for the fall. We were created good but not perfect. When God made us, it wasn't His goal to create equals. All created things are still less than God. Even the angels can fall, and many did. God created good, imperfect people, but perfection is the requirement.

The fall of mankind is a hard story for us to stomach not only because it's so personal but also because of the immeasurable, horrific fallout of the fall. But when I'm able to zoom out on it, I can see how it ushered in the opportunity for Him to rescue us. First Peter 1:18–20 (ESV) says, "You were ransomed from the futile ways inherited from your forefathers, not with perishable things such as silver or gold, but with the precious blood of Christ, like that of a lamb without blemish or spot. He was foreknown before the foundation of the world but was made manifest in the last times for the sake of you."

Third, I believe Scripture teaches that the fall of man makes the larger narrative of the Bible more beautiful. Not on its own, of course. But as the fall plays out in God's bigger story, it makes the rest of the story possible. We see this in Ephesians 1:4–6, which says, "He chose us in him before the foundation of the world, that we should be holy and blameless before him. In love he predestined us for adoption to himself as sons through Jesus Christ, according to the purpose of his will, to the praise of his glorious grace." *"To the praise of his glorious grace!"* Do you see what all this means?

If the fall of man hadn't happened, certain aspects of God's character would have never had a canvas on which to be displayed. The entire universe would miss out on seeing things like how God pursues and even loves His enemies, how He forgives sinners, how He is moved to show mercy and grace. It took time, and it involved His own suffering and humiliation. I can't think of anything more loving than for a Holy God to plan to suffer so that He could redeem a people He hadn't even created yet, who were bound to need His total intervention on their behalf. How incredibly generous and loving!

If it weren't for the fall, we would've missed out on seeing so much of who God is, and we would never be able to revel in the beauty of His redemption. His redemption is a better story than our perfection ever would've been. It shows God as glorious. Through the whole process, we see more of who the three Persons of the Trinity are as they work together in our creation, redemption, and restoration.

Just like all of us, many times God reveals who He is through what He does. And His work of creation, redemption, and restoration shows how engaged He is in this relationship with us—His image bearers, His children. He created you, and He paid for you at His own great expense to buy you back from brokenness. He loves you!

In addition to being created in God's image, Scripture says we are to be conformed to Christ's image. We are born into brokenness, but Scripture doesn't leave us hopeless about our sin nature. Instead, it tells us how to rightly handle our sins. God's Spirit is the one who *brings* conviction *to* our hearts so that we can turn from our sins and walk with God in righteousness. Conviction that produces repentance serves as evidence that He lives in us.

Conforming in Community

Within the context of the body of Christ, a beautiful picture emerges of walking alongside other sinners as we are conformed to His image. No one sins in a vacuum, and because our sin impacts others, it's the kind of thing that is best handled with the greater community in mind.

James, the brother of Jesus, wrote a letter to the church outside of Israel, giving us a glimpse into how Christians can image Christ in their relationships with each other. The final paragraphs of his letter basically say, "You're a sinner. Don't try to hide it. Instead, bring your sin out into the light and ask for help! Tell other people where you struggle; they're strugglers and sinners too. Together, you can ask God to help you because He will. You're not alone in this."

Jesus Leads the Way

Romans 8:29 refers to Jesus as "the firstborn among many brothers." In ancient Jewish culture, the firstborn is the preeminent one—he receives the inheritance and the blessing. But to our great delight, Jesus shares. He, in His position of prominence and perfection, is the reason we can be adopted into God's family. He was the first and only One to perfectly reveal God to humanity in the flesh, but now we all follow His lead, albeit in our humanity and imperfection.

Here's what that looks like when we zoom out on the overall storyline of God's interactions with us:

A. God the Father sent God the Son to earth to show humanity what He is like.

B. God the Son willingly took on the bounds of the earthly realm when He entered into it. He demonstrated the Father's heart to us, showing His compassion, His affection for sinners, His pursuit of our hearts and our joy—not just our adherence to His laws.

C. After fulfilling the Father's demands on our behalf, the incarnate Son returned to the Father in heaven but sent His Spirit to dwell in all His followers so that we might be the demonstration of the Father's heart within the earthly realm.

Through the work of God the Spirit in us, we are one of the primary ways the world sees what God is like. While Scripture and creation reveal Him as well, many people may never read Scripture or acknowledge God as the Creator of the universe, so we have a unique role in revealing Him to those around us. We were created in the flesh, and we are recreated in the Spirit—raised from the dead to "walk in newness of life" (Rom. 6:4–5). This is what new life looks like, to share in Christ's death and resurrection! We love the idea of sharing in His resurrection and life, but the preceding verse (Rom. 6:3) and the following verses talk about sharing in His death too. Take a look at the places both the concepts of life *and* death show up (death-oriented phrases are bolded; life-oriented phrases are underlined):

> For one who has **died** has been <u>set free</u> from sin. Now if we have **died** with Christ, we believe that we will also <u>live</u> with him. We know that Christ, being <u>raised from the dead</u>, will <u>never die again; death no longer has dominion over him</u>. For the **death** he **died** he **died** to sin, once for all, but the <u>life</u> he <u>lives</u> he <u>lives</u> to God. So you also must consider yourselves **dead to sin** and <u>alive to God</u> in Christ Jesus. (Rom. 6:7–11, emphasis added)

Scripture gives us snapshots of many ways we're being conformed to the image of Christ through the process of our life, death, and resurrection.

- We are sent like Him (John 20:21–22).
- We suffer like Him (Heb. 13:12–13).
- We identify with Him (John 15:8).
- We will be resurrected like Him (1 Cor. 15:49).
- We will be transformed like Him (Phil. 3:20–21).
- We will be glorified with Him (Rom. 8:17).

How can these things be possible for us, mere humans? And how will we endure the more trying aspects of these things? Scripture also has good news—shocking news—for us along these lines. Not only does God the Spirit live in us, but all three Persons of the eternal triune God live in us! But don't take my word for it; look up these Bible passages in your own study time if you'd like and be amazed:

- God the Father lives in us (John 14:23; 1 John 4:12, 16).
- God the Son lives in us (John 14:18–20; 15:4–5; Gal. 2:20; Eph. 3:17).
- And God the Spirit lives in us (John 14:17; Rom. 8:11; 1 Cor. 6:19).

This reaffirms one of the most comforting, beautiful truths of Scripture: God is not tentative about us. He is not hedging His bets—one foot in relationship, the other out the door. He has set His heart fully on us; He is completely bought in and has already paid the full price. We are eternally guarded by God's presence in our lives. As such, this reinforces our eternal security. Having His nature and His presence marks our adoption into His family. I love how Donald Macleod sums it up:

> Christ is God's Son eternally: we become God's sons and daughters only when we receive Jesus (John 1:12). He is God's Son by nature; we become God's children by grace (1 John 3:1). But the relationship itself is

essentially the same. We are heirs of God and
co-heirs with Christ (Rom. 8:17). We have
exactly the same inheritance. According to
John 17:26, we are loved with the same love.[3]

What a stunning truth! Not only are we conformed to the
image of Christ, but we are loved with the same love as Christ,
indwelled by the triune God, and empowered to demonstrate
the goodness of God to the world around us—to every person
who crosses our path. We were created in the flesh, and we are
recreated in the Spirit.

Whether you're seventeen or seventy-five, there is a call on
your life—to demonstrate God to the world around you. You
have a unique sphere of influence and are uniquely gifted by
the Spirit to fulfill your calling. And just as the Spirit empowered Jesus for ministry, He also empowers you. He will equip
you to obey Him. You don't have to muster the strength on
your own—ask Him for help. Ask Him to guide you, to give
you words, to open the right doors widely and close the wrong
doors tightly. Ask Him to direct your steps and strengthen
you for the journey. He stands ready to help you always. You're
not in this alone. Philippians 2:13 says God is the one who is
working in you to desire to do good and then to actually do
it. He is at work in you! And on the days you feel like you're
the first to battle through the hardships that come with demonstrating who God is to a lost and broken world, remember,
Jesus led the way long before you were ever called to such a

task! He has gone before you, and He will help you follow in His footsteps.

Imitators of Christ (To Make the Father Known)

One of the supernatural by-products of being redeemed by God and conformed to the image of Christ is that we will begin to act like Him. Our internal transformation is revealed. This is what Jesus was referring to when He said, "By this my Father is glorified, that you bear much fruit and so prove to be my disciples" (John 15:8).

Just as Jesus walked in obedience to the Father (John 15:10) through this continual abiding, God's abiding in us means we're able to walk in a unique kind of power over sin and the flesh (Rom. 8:37; Phil. 4:13). This power calls us to be mindful of our eternal purposes, to walk by the Spirit and not by the flesh, since both the power and glory of the eternal God dwells in us. To summarize Macleod, God is always in our space, which means every sin we commit is committed "under his very nose." And yet when we do sin, He does not leave us or forsake us. In fact, we would have no power over sin if He did leave us. He knows He is our only hope for change, because He is the One who equips us to imitate Christ.

According to Scripture, God's kindness leads us to repentance (Rom. 2:4), and He is the one who grants us repentance (2 Tim. 2:25). We are able to obey God when He prompts repentance because He has given us a new spirit and a new heart (Ezek. 36:26–27), and His Spirit in us moves us toward obedience.

We've seen how the Persons of the Trinity are uniquely and unitedly involved in our creation and salvation. In the same way, they continue to participate in our sanctification—working together toward the goal of conforming us to the image of Christ. The Spirit of Christ is working in you to recreate in you the same beautiful things you see in Jesus!

Michael Reeves said, "Christianity is not primarily about lifestyle change; it is about knowing God."[4] He also said, "What we love and enjoy is foundationally important. It is far more significant than our outward behaviour, for it is our desires that *drive* our behaviour. We do what we want."[5]

Centuries earlier, the French philosopher Blaise Pascal said it this way:

> All men seek happiness. This is without exception. Whatever different means they employ, they all tend to this end. The cause of some going to war, and of others avoiding it, is the same desire in both, attended with different views. The will never takes the least step but to this object. This is the motive of every action of every man, even of those who hang themselves.[6]

We do what we want. We all seek our own happiness. In light of this, it's important to ask ourselves: *What do we want? What do we love? And where do we believe happiness is found?*

Ephesians 5:1–2 calls us to be imitators of Christ: "Therefore be imitators of God, as beloved children. And walk in love, as Christ loved us and gave himself up for us, a fragrant offering and sacrifice to God."

Why would we want to imitate Him? Or anyone? We imitate what we find beautiful and desirable. When you see someone with shoes you like, you probably wish you had them too. Maybe you even want to go buy those shoes for yourself. And even beyond that, when you find something you love, you want others to love it too. We want the world to find what we've found, so we talk about it and spread the word. We put bumper stickers on our cars, wear logos on our T-shirts, and generally become walking commercials for things we want to be associated with. We are always pointing to something beyond ourselves, but nothing we point to is eternal unless it is God Himself. Everything else will fall apart or fade out of fashion.

As we aim to imitate Christ, what specifically should we imitate? I've heard comedians talk about what it's like to do an impression of someone else: they say you first have to pick up on the things that stand out about her most before you move to the subtle nuances. You emphasize her drawl or her famous hand gestures or a phrase she repeats often.

When you think about Jesus, perhaps you think about His resurrection or His miracles—His actions. But if you zoom in on the character and personality that lies underneath all of His actions, one thing stands out to me as His most noteworthy attribute: *Jesus is known for His love.* Love has always been true of the Persons of the Trinity throughout all eternity. And in fact, it's what He calls us to imitate about Him: "Love one another as I have loved you" (John 15:12).

Take heart—you aren't called to imitate His ability to walk on water or turn it into wine. You're called to love. But sometimes that seems even harder, doesn't it? Somehow, bending the laws of nature feels less challenging than speaking loving words to the family member who voices his/her disapproval of all your decisions. Or showing love to the stranger online whose political opinions grate against the core of your personal beliefs. When faced with the call to love those people, you may feel more equipped to raise Lazarus from the dead!

Loving others is hard work, but loving only yourself is a godless, joyless endeavor. As Tim Keller said in his book *The Reason for God*, "Nothing makes us more miserable than self-absorption, the endless, unsmiling concentration on our needs, wants, treatment, ego, and record."[7] The good news is: if you struggle to love people well, you don't have to do it on your own. You don't have to muster up love or fake it. In fact, you can't. So how do you do it?

Here's what it looks like to imitate God and His love. First, remember that God has generously, abundantly poured out His love to you. Because of that, you can dial into the love you've received from Him; you can remember His patience and compassion toward you. Second, as you recall His love toward you, you can ask Him to ignite that same love in your own heart as you engage with Him to respond to those who are difficult for you to love. They aren't difficult for Him to love. And He actually lives inside you and promises to guide you! Don't be surprised if you feel the Spirit prompting you with an idea: *Here's how you do it*. It's kind of like having the golf pro stand with you and put his hands over your hands and do the swing for you.

As we imitate God, it's important to remember that we don't imitate Him in order to impress Him. He knows what He's like, and He knows what we're like (Ps. 103:14). And He knows the only way we can imitate Him is through His work in us. He gets the glory, and we get the joy. Ultimately, we imitate Him because He's the path to joy—for us and for others!

In his letter to the church in Thessalonica, Paul reminded believers that they were children of light and called them to live in the light. God destined His children for salvation, not for wrath. Paul charged the church to encourage one another with reminders of this regularly (1 Thess. 5:11). When we forget who we are, it's easy to walk in a false identity. But as God's children of light who imitate Christ who is the Light (John 1:4, 9–10; 8:12), we can live a different story. We can live the truth instead of the lie.

Paul marked out what that looks like for us: showing respect, being at peace, meeting people where they are in the space of whatever needs they have—whether it's encouragement or help or admonishment (1 Thess. 5:12–14). And in all of those spaces of need, he reminded them to rejoice and pray and give thanks. He says, "This is God's will for you"—to rejoice always, pray without ceasing, and give thanks in all circumstances (vv. 16–18). These admonitions make a lot of sense, for when we do them, we look a lot like Jesus!

Paul also instructed them, "Do not quench the Spirit" (v. 19). The Spirit is our Guide, our reminder of who we are as God's beloved children. We quench His work in our lives when we don't follow His lead or when we live out of a false identity. But when we follow Him just as Jesus did in His earthly ministry, we walk in the light. We use our access to His strength in order to shake off sin and temptation and walk in freedom.

This is the path of our sanctification, the process where God continually conforms us to the image of His Son. While He has already declared us righteous because of the finished work of Christ—that's called "justification"—He's working now to form Christ's righteousness in us—that's called "sanctification." Both justification and sanctification are things God does—to us, in us, and for us. Paul said, "May the God of peace himself sanctify you completely" (1 Thess. 5:23). And Paul leaves his readers with this encouraging reminder, "He who calls you is faithful; he will surely do it" (v. 24).

The Body of Christ

The Persons of the Trinity work together to accomplish the redemptive plan for humanity, which serves as a great reminder for us that we're designed to do our best work in community. As much as God is at work in you, you alone aren't capable of demonstrating His love in all the ways necessary to reveal Him to a world in need. First of all, you have to sleep at some point. Second, you can only be in one place at a time. And third, you're limited in your finances, resources, and skills. Fortunately, God has already pieced all these things together. In chapter 4 ("God the Spirit"), we talked about the various spiritual gifts God has given us and how they serve to benefit the church. We don't all have all the gifts, which means we need one another! God lovingly planted us in a family of Christ followers, the church, and as we work together in unity with our unique skills and passions, we demonstrate His love to a watching world!

Scripture calls us to remember that we are united with one another. We are a body with many members (Rom. 12:4–5; 1 Cor. 12:27), and He is the head of the body (Col. 1:18). The church is the body of Christ because we are united with the body of Christ. And Jesus longed for and prayed for us to be united with one another in the same kind of unity He shares with us and with the Father.

In a prayer Jesus prayed to the Father, He referenced all who will believe in Him across the whole course of history, including you! And what did He want for you and for all other believers? Just look at how many times you see the word "one" or "in" within this passage, and it becomes clear: Jesus wanted *unity* for us. He wants us to be *one* to the same level He and the Father are one.

> "I do not ask for these only, but also for those who will believe in me through their word, that they may all be **one**, just as you, Father, are **in** me, and I **in** you, that they also may be **in** us, so that the world may believe that you have sent me. The glory that you have given me I have given to them, that they may be **one** even as we are **one, I in** them and you **in** me, that they may become perfectly **one,** so that the world may know that you sent me and loved them even as you loved me." (John 17:20–23 emphasis added)

Our unity with each other stems from the fact that we all have the same relationship to God. Every other Christian is our brother or sister in Christ, chosen and adopted by Him into His family. And we all are indwelled by Him. In fact, we are not just individually the dwelling place of God, but the church itself is the dwelling place of God. Ephesians 2:18–22 describes us as a building God is establishing—with Jesus as its cornerstone, "in whom the whole structure, being joined together, grows into a holy temple in the Lord. In him you also are being built together into a dwelling place for God by the Spirit" (vv. 21–22). As eternal family, we're not only inextricably joined with Him but with each other too. And to be fair, "joined" is probably too small a word to capture the dynamics and dimensions of this relationship—we are fused, grafted into it.

Just as in any other relationship, there will be times when we will face challenges. We can expect our unity to face threats from both internal and external sources. The early church was no stranger to these threats. In Paul's encouragement-filled letter to the church at Philippi, he spent a lot of time reminding them of the beauty and joy that comes from knowing God, from seeing how that impacts the whole church community. One of the things the Holy Spirit does as He lives in all believers is help create peace and unity among us. He works in each individually but also for the good of the whole.

Paul went on to say we should live in harmony in the midst of suffering (Phil. 2:14–16). This is important because suffering can bring out the worst in you. It can prompt you to be short-tempered and selfish and live from a scarcity mentality. But Paul reminds the church to count others as more significant—not equal but better—and to look to serve their interests. That's what Jesus did, after all (Phil. 2:3–7).

In his letter to the church at Ephesus, Paul urged Christ followers to be humble. Humility, gentleness, patience, love, and peace were signs that the members of the church were walking in their calling. He urged them to use their gifts to serve the church because serving would help mature them in the faith.

He called them to live differently, and he gave examples of the ways God's Spirit transforms us and makes us new: we take off lies and put on truth. We take off selfish anger and put on peacemaking. We take off stealing and put on sharing. We take off foolishness and put on wisdom. We take off darkness and put on light. We take off drunkenness and put on Spirit-filled praise. We take off sinful words and put on encouraging words (4:1–3, 25–32).

He repeatedly addressed our use of words. Words should be treated like gifts—gifts of grace, specifically. Nobody wants a bad gift, so he said we should do away with those—corrupting talk, bitterness, wrath, anger, clamor, slander, malice, filthiness, foolish talk, and crude joking. On the other hand, gifts of grace are words that build up and show kindness—words of tenderheartedness, forgiveness, and thanksgiving (4:29–32).

Christ modeled how we should treat one another and speak to one another. There is freedom and joy in following His lead, even when—or especially when—it goes against our nature.

First John 4:7–21 reveals deep truths about God's love, and it is bookended with an important detail: God is deeply invested in the way we love *one another*. God's love for us not only reveals how we should love (4:17), but it also compels us to love (4:7–8, 11, 21). Just as God is outgoing in His love, we should be too! We are deeply involved with Him and with one another on every level of kingdom life, though it's often challenging to remember this and live it out.

The picture Scripture paints is one where Christ followers of various tribal, political, and socioeconomic backgrounds live together with Christ as their focus. Among Jesus's disciples, He had the wealthy tax collector and the poor fishermen; He had one who worked for Rome and one who wanted to overthrow Rome. He welcomed those who were considered filthy and godless—pagans, prostitutes, and lepers—and their eternities changed because of who He is, not who they were. These people are our eternal family members.

What a beautiful demonstration not only of His love and unity but of His diversity! Not only did Jesus live in this way, but His followers did too. The early church, made up primarily of circumcised Jews, began to see an influx of Gentile followers after the coming of the Holy Spirit, but they didn't demand circumcision of them (Acts 15:1–21). Their primary concern was that their shared belief in Jesus not be disrupted by division. But this definitely wasn't a seamless process. Change can be difficult for any of us, especially where religious beliefs are concerned, and it often results in conflict as people adjust. That's what happened with the early church. They had to get through some bumpy times to throw open the doors of the gospel. Even the leaders struggled at times. In fact, Paul had to call out Peter when he caved to peer pressure and disregarded the Gentile believers, choosing to eat only with the Jewish believers. Paul rebuked him for showing partiality, which is divisive (Gal. 2:11–14).

Jesus spent more time identifying Himself with His church as a whole than with any one individual. For instance, prior to his conversion to Christianity, the apostle Paul was an outspoken persecutor of Christians. When the voice of the resurrected, ascended Christ spoke from heaven and confronted Paul about his actions, He asked, "Why are you persecuting me?" (Acts 9:4). Jesus was already back in heaven, but He was identifying Himself with the persecution of the church. Additionally, Scripture calls Jesus "the head of the body" (Col. 1:18), and the head certainly knows and experiences all the body endures.

The New Testament repeatedly affirms the connection between the unity of the church and the triune life of God. Just as God's unity and diversity are revealed in His triune nature, we participate in the triune life through the Son, being united in Him in our diversity. Donald Macleod said, "We must be careful not to set this unity and this diversity over against each other. The church is not one *despite* its diversity but *because* of its diversity."[8] This is harmony not homogeny. Every person playing the same instrument with the same note does not make a symphony. But different instruments hitting different notes to the same rhythm and key of the same song? That's beautiful! The **Economic Trinity** has demonstrated this for us, working out a unified will and purpose through distinct roles to accomplish it. This is love.

As the people who are made in His image, conformed to His image, and called to imitate Him, we should expect

that others will be drawn to Him through our lives and witness! The love that rescued us is pursuing others who don't
yet know Him, and He's using us as His ambassadors in that
process.

When we recall that God loved us with an outgoing love,
we are reminded that love doesn't keep the good news of the
gospel to itself. It shares—even with people who are different
from us in every way. Because that's what He did. Just as God
demonstrates His unity and diversity through the Trinity, we
demonstrate His unity and diversity through the body. When
others see our relationship with God, our hope is that they'll
want to have that relationship too!

Continued Growth

Jesus commanded His disciples to make disciples. The
word *disciple* means "learner."[9] He wanted the learners to
learn, then teach. He told them to baptize the new disciples,
but He didn't just say to baptize them in His own name—He
said to baptize them in the name of the Father, and of the Son,
and of the Holy Spirit. We are baptized into Christ—buried
and raised with Him—and this is how we participate in the
communion of the Trinity. Our verbal confession and action
of being baptized are important, but we need to understand
that baptism is fundamentally about who we are. It's about our
union with the triune God.

Since many professing believers know very little about the
three Persons of the Trinity, we have failed terribly at obeying

Jesus's command in our lives and in our churches. It's vital that the doctrine of the Trinity not be glossed over but be widely taught and understood among professing Christians. That's one of the reasons it's so important that you're reading this book!

As we wrap up, I want to touch on an important reminder: **The Trinity is central to the gospel.** The glory of God shines brightest when the gospel is demonstrated through Christ's death and resurrection. Despite the spotlight being on Christ in that moment, our salvation and redemption would have never been attainable without all three distinct Persons of God being involved in the process. Jesus saves—and He saves not only through His finished work on the cross but in partnership with the initiating power of the Father and the sustaining power of the Spirit. Not to mention what happens on the other side of our salvation: once we are saved *out of* sin and death, we're saved *into* relationship not with one Person but with the triune God!

I hope this will be a launching pad for you to dig deeper into the Word—to read all of it if you haven't. And if you have, to do it again and forever. Keep looking for Him—Father, Son, and Spirit—every day for the rest of your life!

Our new, richer understanding of who God is will begin to inform everything about the way we make peace with our past, live in the present, look to the future, and interact with others around us. Knowing Him better changes the way we know ourselves. Knowing Him better changes the way we love others. Now that we see Him more clearly, we can confidently say: He's where the joy is!

Glossary

Christophany: a manifestation of the pre-incarnate Christ[1]

Consubstantial: regarded as the same in substance or essence[2]

Doctrine: Christian teaching on a specific subject[3]

Economic Trinity: the external work of the Trinity (as it relates to creation and humanity)[4]

Glorify: to show as worthy, to praise, to appreciate, to serve, to please[5]

Hypostatic Union: the doctrine of the two natures, divine and human, in the single person of Jesus Christ[6]

Immanent Trinity: the internal life of the triune God[7]

Monotheism: belief in the one true God who is the sovereign Creator[8]

Polytheism: belief in many gods[9]

Progressive Revelation: God didn't reveal His whole plan for His people at one time. He worked through His process via different means, patiently giving us more information piece by piece, at just the right time.[10]

Theology: a set of beliefs about God.[11] We all have beliefs about God, so you're already a theologian! Our goal is to be good theologians who believe true things about God that are consistent with Scripture. That means we'll always be adding to (and sometimes adjusting) what we know about God as we search Scripture and learn more of what it teaches us about God.

Theophany: any appearance of God in Scripture that humans can perceive with their senses; predominantly used to describe visible revealings[12]

Heresies

A heresy is any belief or teaching that denies one or more of the foundational truths about God. These are some of the heresies denying Scripture's teachings about the Father, Son, and/or Spirit.

Arianism: a heresy denying that Jesus is truly God; denied Christ's full divinity, stating that Christ was a created being who was superior to human beings but inferior to God[1]

Docetism: a heresy that says Jesus wasn't actually human but only appeared to be human[2]

Gnosticism: a heresy that says the body and all physical things are corrupt so Jesus could not really be human[3]

Henotheism: a heresy that says the god(s) in charge vary at different locations around the world or for different people groups[4]

Modalism: a heresy that says God is one person who appears to us in three different forms rather than three distinct Persons ("Jesus Only," "Jesus Name Movement," and "Oneness Pentecostalism" are associated with this.)[5]

Monarchianism: a heresy that stresses the unity of God so heavily that it discounts God's plurality as three distinct Persons[6]

Monophysitism: a heresy that says Jesus's divinity fully absorbed His humanity so that, in the end, He was only divine and not human[7]

Nestorianism: a heresy that says Jesus was a human person who was joined to the divine Son of God[8]

Polytheism: a heresy that says there are many gods[9]

Subordinationism: a heresy that says Jesus is not created, but He is still inferior to the Father, and thus not equal to the Father in being and attributes[10]

Tritheism: a heresy that says the Trinity consists of three separate Gods[11] (Many groups who reject the Trinity often falsely accuse or misunderstand those who believe in the Trinity as holding this position.)

Unitarianism: a heresy that says God is only one Person instead of three Persons[12]

Athanasian Creed

We've included the Athanasian Creed as a reference document because it is the most definitive statement on the Trinity from the early church. The origin of the creed likely goes back to the late fifth century. It affirms that "all members of the Godhead are considered uncreated and coeternal and of the same substance."[1]

> We worship one God in trinity and the
>   trinity in unity,
> neither blending their persons
> nor dividing their essence.
>   For the person of the Father is a distinct
>   person,
>   the person of the Son is another,
>   and that of the Holy Spirit still another.
>   But the divinity of the Father, Son, and
>   Holy Spirit is one,
>   their glory equal, their majesty coeternal.

What quality the Father has, the Son has,
    and the Holy Spirit has.
The Father is uncreated,
the Son is uncreated,
the Holy Spirit is uncreated.

The Father is immeasurable,
the Son is immeasurable,
the Holy Spirit is immeasurable.

The Father is eternal,
the Son is eternal,
the Holy Spirit is eternal.

    And yet there are not three eternal
beings;
        there is but one eternal being.
    So too there are not three uncreated
or immeasurable beings;
        there is but one uncreated and
immeasurable being.

Similarly, the Father is almighty,
    the Son is almighty,
    the Holy Spirit is almighty.
        Yet there are not three almighty
    beings;
        there is but one almighty being.

Thus the Father is God,
the Son is God,
the Holy Spirit is God.

> Yet there are not three gods;
> there is but one God.

Thus the Father is Lord,
the Son is Lord,
the Holy Spirit is Lord.

> Yet there are not three lords;
> there is but one Lord.

Just as Christian truth compels us
to confess each person individually
as both God and Lord,
so catholic religion forbids us
to say that there are three gods or lords.

The Father was neither made nor created
nor begotten from anyone.
The Son was neither made nor created;
he was begotten from the Father alone.
The Holy Spirit was neither made nor
created nor begotten;
he proceeds from the Father and the Son.

Accordingly there is one Father, not three
fathers;
there is one Son, not three sons;

there is one Holy Spirit, not three holy
spirits.

Nothing in this trinity is before or after,
nothing is greater or smaller;
in their entirety the three persons
are coeternal and coequal with each
other.

So in everything, as was said earlier,
we must worship their trinity in their
unity
and their unity in their trinity.

Anyone then who desires to be saved

should think thus about the trinity.

But it is necessary for eternal salvation
that one also believe in the incarnation
of our Lord Jesus Christ faithfully.

Now this is the true faith:

That we believe and confess
that our Lord Jesus Christ, God's Son,
is both God and human, equally.

He is God from the essence of the
Father,
begotten before time;

and he is human from the essence of his
mother,
born in time;
completely God, completely human,
with a rational soul and human flesh;
equal to the Father as regards divinity,
less than the Father as regards humanity.

Although he is God and human,
yet Christ is not two, but one.
He is one, however,
not by his divinity being turned into
flesh,
but by God's taking humanity to himself.
He is one,
certainly not by the blending of his
essence,
but by the unity of his person.
For just as one human is both rational
soul and flesh,
so too the one Christ is both God and
human.
He suffered for our salvation;
he descended to hell;
he arose from the dead;
he ascended to heaven;
he is seated at the Father's right hand;

from there he will come to judge the
living and the dead.

At his coming all people will arise bodily
and give an accounting of their own
deeds.

Those who have done good will enter
eternal life, and those who have done evil
will enter eternal fire.[2]

Further Study

I want to extend my deep gratitude to the following preachers and teachers who have greatly contributed to my knowledge of the Trinity (and therefore to the content of this book):

Tim Keller

Fred Sanders

Michael Reeves

R. C. Sproul

John Piper

Wayne Grudem

J. R. Vassar

Bruce Ware

Sam Allberry

James R. White

Donald Macleod

Other Books on the Trinity

For a simple, straightforward overview:

> *Shared Life: The Trinity and the Fellowship of God's People* by Donald Macleod

General overview:

> *The Deep Things of God: How the Trinity Changes Everything* by Fred Sanders

For historical context:

> *The Holy Trinity: In Scripture, History, Theology, and Worship* by Robert Letham

For an exploration of the original language:

> *The Forgotten Trinity: Recovering the Heart of Christian Belief* by James R. White

In relation to other world religions:

> *Delighting in the Trinity: An Introduction to the Christian Faith* by Michael Reeves

Notes

Introduction

1. J. I. Packer, *Concise Theology: A Guide to Historic Christian Beliefs* (Wheaton: Tyndale House, 1993), 40.

2. Augustine is sometimes credited with this.

3. "History of Trinitarian Doctrines," Stanford Encyclopedia of Philosophy, accessed April 21, 2021, https://plato.stanford.edu/entries/trinity/trinity-history.html.

4. Ligon Duncan, "How Is the Trinity Central to the Gospel?" TGC, October 4, 2017, accessed May 5, 2021, https://www.thegospel-coalition.org/video/trinity-central-gospel.

Chapter 1: Unity and Diversity

1. Thomas Aquinas, *Theological Texts* (Oxford: University Press, 1955), 295.

2. Matt Perman, "What Is the Doctrine of the Trinity," Desiring God, January 23, 2006, accessed April 21, 2021, https://www.desiring-god.org/articles/what-is-the-doctrine-of-the-trinity.

3. B. B. Warfield, as quoted by Justin Taylor in "B. B. Warfield's Analogy for the Trinity in the Old Testament," April 18, 2017, accessed April 26, 2021, https://www.thegospelcoalition.org/blogs/justin-taylor/b-b--warfields-analogy-for-the-trinity-in-the-old-testament.

4. Strong's H430, Blue Letter Bible, accessed April 26, 2021, https://www.blueletterbible.org/lang/lexicon/lexicon.cfm?t=kjv&strongs=h430.

5. Donald Macleod, *Shared Life: The Trinity and the Fellowship of God's People* (Fearn, Ross-shire, UK: Christian Focus Publications, 2005), 13.

6. Wayne Grudem, *Systematic Theology* (Grand Rapids, MI: Zondervan, 1994), 255.

7. James R. White, *The Forgotten Trinity: Recovering the Heart of Christian Belief* (Ada, MI: Baker Books, 2019).

8. Fred Sanders, *The Deep Things of God: How the Trinity Changes Everything* (Wheaton, IL: Crossway, 2017), 68.

9. Tim Keller, "The Triune God," Gospel in Life, June 12, 2011, https://gospelinlife.com/downloads/the-triune-god-4908.

10. *Oxford Dictionary*, s.v. "immanent," accessed April 26, 2021, https://www.lexico.com/en/definition/immanent.

11. Sanders, *The Deep Things of God*.

12. Sanders, *The Deep Things of God*, 89.

13. Strong's G3621, *Blue Letter Bible*, accessed April 21, 2021, https://www.blueletterbible.org/lang/lexicon/lexicon.cfm?t=kjv&strongs=g362.

14. Sanders, *The Deep Things of God*.

15. Tim Keller, "The Glory of the Triune God," Gospel in Life, June 19, 2011, accessed May 5, 2021, https://gospelinlife.com/downloads/the-triune-god-4908.

Chapter 2: God the Father

1. Michael Reeves, *Delighting in the Trinity: An Introduction to the Christian Faith* (Downers Grove, IL: IVP Academic, 2012), 111.

2. J. I. Packer, *Knowing God* (Downers Grove, IL: IVP Books, 1973), 201.

3. Fred Sanders, *The Deep Things of God: How the Trinity Changes Everything* (Wheaton, IL: Crossway, 2017).

4. Jonathan Edwards, *A Treatise Concerning Religious Affections* (Glasgow: W. Collins & Co., 1840), 77.

5. Reeves, *Delighting in the Trinity*.

6. "The Most Quoted Verse in the Bible," *Character of God*, Episode 1, Bible Project Podcast, August 17, 2020, https://bibleproject.com/podcast/most-quoted-verse-bible.

7. "Overview of Food Ingredients, Additives & Color," FDA, November 2004, revised April 2010, https://www.fda.gov/food/

food-ingredients-packaging/overview-food-ingredients-additives-colors#:~:text=Food%20manufacturers%20are%20required%20 to,by%20those%20in%20smaller%20amounts.

Chapter 3: God the Son

1. Bill Cook, *40 Days in Mark* (Nashville, TN: B&H Publishing, 2020).

2. Don Stewart, "What Does the Hebrew Term *Adonai* Stand For?," Blue Letter Bible, accessed April 12, 2021, https://www.blueletterbible. org/Comm/stewart_don/faq/the-attributes-of-god-that-belong-to-him-alone/21-what-does-the-hebrew-term-adonai-stand-for.cfm.

3. *Nicene Creed*, accessed April 13, 2021, via https://www.marquette.edu/faith/prayers-nicene.php.

4. *Nicene Creed*, accessed April 13, 2021, via https://www.marquette.edu/faith/prayers-nicene.php.

5. Strong's G3056, *Blue Letter Bible*, accessed April 12, 2021, https://www. blueletterbible.org/lang/lexicon/lexicon.cfm?Strongs=G3056&t=KJV.

6. Richard R. Melick Jr., *New American Commentary: Philippians, Colossians, Philemon*, vol. 32 (Nashville: B&H, 1991), 217.

7. Tim Chaffey, "Theophanies in the Old Testament," Answers in Genesis, January 13, 2012, https://answersingenesis.org/jesus/incarnation/theophanies-in-the-old-testament.

8. Strong's H43397, *Blue Letter Bible*, accessed April 12, 2021, https://www.blueletterbible.org/lang/lexicon/lexicon.cfm?Strongs= H4397&t=KJV.

9. John Owen, *The Person and Glory of Christ* (New York: Robert Carter & Brothers, 1852), 349–50.

10. Need source information.

11. Fred Sanders, *The Deep Things of God : How the Trinity Changes Everything* (Wheaton, IL: Crossway, 2017).

12. David Mathis, "What Is the Hypostatic Union?," desiringGod, December 19, 2007, https://www.desiringgod.org/articles/what-is-the-hypostatic-union.

13. Ulrik Nissen, *The Polity of Christ : Studies on Dietrich Bonhoeffer's Chalcedonian Christology and Ethics* (London: T&T Clark, Bloomsbury Publishing, 2020), 16.

14. R. C. Sproul, *The Work of Christ : What the Events of Jesus' Life Means for You* (Colorado Springs: David C. Cook, 2012), 8.

15. Martin Luther, *Luther's Works: Reformation Writings and Occasional Pieces* (St. Louis: Concordia, 1955), 316.

16. C. S. Lewis, *Mere Christianity*, accessed August 23, 2023, https://www.dacc.edu/assets/pdfs/PCM/merechristianitylewis.pdf.

17. Robert Letham, "The Ascension of Christ," The Gospel Coalition, accessed August 23, 2023, https://www.thegospelcoalition. org/essay/ascension-of-christ.

Chapter 4: God the Spirit

1. Strong's H7307, *Blue Letter Bible*, accessed April 15, 2021, https://www.blueletterbible.org/lang/lexicon/lexicon.cfm?t=kjv& strongs=h7307.

2. Strong's G4151, *Blue Letter Bible*, accessed April 15, 2021, https://www.blueletterbible.org/lang/lexicon/lexicon. cfm?t=kjv&strongs=g4151.

3. James B. Torrance, *Worship, Community and the Triune Grace of God* (Downers Grove, IL: InterVarsity Press, 1996), 76.

4. Andy Naselli, "The Unpardonable Sin," The Gospel Coalition, accessed April 15, 2021, https://www.thegospelcoalition.org/essay/ the-unpardonable-sin.

5. "The Illustrious History of Signet Rings," Berganza, accessed August 24, 2023, https://www.berganza.com/feature-history-of-sig- net-rings.html.

Chapter 5: Prayer and Communication

1. Tim Keller, Twitter, February 23, 2015, accessed April 19, 2021, https://twitter.com/timkellernyc/status/569890726349307904?lang =en.

2. Tim Chester, *Delighting in the Trinity* (London: The Good Book Company, 2010).

3. Sam Allberry, "The Trinity and Christian Prayer," The Village Church, interview, April 12, 2015, https://5zu3o1glj423bhz11le70nbe- wpengine.netdna-ssl.com/wp-content/uploads/2020/04/2015041211 15FMWC21ASAAA_SamAllberry-TheTrinityandChristianPrayer. pdf.

4. Sam Allberry, "The Trinity and Christian Prayer."

5. Sam Allberry, "The Trinity and Christian Prayer."

6. C. S. Lewis, "Letter 21," *Letters to Malcolm: Chiefly on Prayer* (San Francisco: HarperOne, 2017, originally pub. 1963 by Harcourt Brace).

7. John Piper, as quoted by Jared Wilson in *Gospel-Driven Ministry: An Introduction to the Calling and Work of a Pastor* (Grand Rapids, MI: Zondervan, 2021), 50.

8. Fred Sanders, *The Deep Things of God: How the Trinity Changes Everything* (Wheaton, IL: Crossway, 2017), 85.

9. Gerald Bray, as quoted by Sanders in *The Triune God* (Grand Rapids, MI: Zondervan, 2016).

10. Regarding the Jewish expectation for the Messiah to overthrow Rome, see https://www.thegospelcoalition.org/commentary/psalm-1-psalm-41/. See https://www.christianity.com/wiki/jesus-christ/why-was-the-messiah-expected-to-free-israel-from-rome.html. See https://www.thegospelcoalition.org/essay/the-messianic-hope/.

11. Timothy Keller, *Prayer: Experiencing Awe and Intimacy with God* (New York: Penguin, 2014), 229.

12. James B. Torrance, *Worship, Community, and the Triune God of Grace* (Downers Grove, IL: InterVarsity Press, 1996), 15.

13. Emilie Griffin, *Clinging: The Experience of Prayer* (Wichita, KS: Eighth Day Press, 2003), 7–8.

14. John Piper, *When I Don't Desire God: How to Fight for Joy* (Wheaton, IL: Crossway, 2004), 167.

Chapter 6: In His Image

1. Richard Sibbes, as quoted by Fred Sanders, *The Deep Things of God: How the Trinity Changes Everything* (Wheaton, IL: Crossway, 2017).

2. Donald Macleod, *Shared Life: The Trinity and the Fellowship of God's People* (Fearn, Ross-shire, Scotland: Christian Focus Publications, 2005), 58–59.

3. Macleod, *Shared Life*, 87.

4. Michael Reeves, *Delighting in the Trinity: An Introduction to the Christian Faith* (Downers Grove, IL: IVP Academic, 2012), 10.

5. Michael Reeves, *The Good God: Enjoying Father, Son, and Spirit* (Milton Keynes, UK: Paternoster, 2012).

6. Blaise Pascal, *Pensées* (New York: P. F. Collier & Son, 1910), 138.

7. Tim Keller, *The Reason for God: Belief in an Age of Skepticism* (New York: Penguin Books, 2018), 229.

8. Macleod, *Shared Life*, 79.

9. Strong's G3101, *Blue Letter Bible*, accessed April 23, 2021, https://www.blueletterbible.org/lang/lexicon/lexicon.cfm?t=esv&strongs=g3101.

Glossary

1. Ligon Duncan, in a sermon on Genesis 32:24–32 entitled "A Stormy Walk-Clinging to God," given on December 5, 1999 (https://ligonduncan.com/a-stormy-walk-clinging-to-god-1010/). Also, see Todd A. Wilson's CHRISTOPHANY note in Week 4 of his TGC/Crossway study on the book of Daniel: "Although God the Son did not make his dwelling among us in the flesh until the time of the incarnation, the Old Testament provides a number of suggestive anticipations of the incarnation, when a human figure suddenly appears on the scene in the service of God. Analogous to a theophany, scholars call these episodes Christophanies, literally, Christ-appearings. Perhaps the most intriguing is found in Genesis 18, when the Lord appears to Abraham and talks to him (Gen. 18:1–2; see also Gen. 32:22–32). Many students of the Bible believe we have another Christophany . . . in Daniel 3, with the sudden appearance of this one who is like 'a son of the gods' (v. 25) and rescues Daniel's three friends."

Daniel: A 12-Week Study © 2015 by Todd A. Wilson. All rights reserved. Used by permission of Crossway Books, a publishing ministry of Good News Publishers (https://www.thegospelcoalition.org/course/knowing-the-bible-daniel/#week-4-nebuchadnezzar-builds-a-great-statue-31-30).

2. *Merriam-Webster*, s.v. "consubstantial," accessed April 26, 2021, https://www.merriam-webster.com/dictionary/consubstantial.

3. Don Stewart, "What Is Christian Teaching?," *Blue Letter Bible*, accessed April 26, 2021, https://www.blueletterbible.org/Comm/stewart_don/faq/bible-basics/question2-what-is-christian-doctrine.cfm.

4. "What Is the Economic and Immanent Trinity?," *Zondervan Academic*, April 27, 2018, https://zondervanacademic.com/blog/what-is-the-economic-and-immanent-trinity.

5. *Merriam-Webster*, s.v. "glorify," accessed April 26, 2021. https://www.merriam-webster.com/dictionary/glorify.

6. David Mathis, "What Is the Hypostatic Union?," desiringGod, December 19, 2007, https://www.desiringgod.org/articles/what-is-the-hypostatic-union.

7. "What Is the Economic and Immanent Trinity?," *Zondervan Academic*.

8. Don Stewart, "What Is a Monotheistic Religion?," *Blue Letter Bible*, accessed April 26, 2021, https://www.blueletterbible.org/faq/don_stewart/don_stewart_299.cfm.

9. Don Stewart, "What Is Polytheism?," *Blue Letter Bible*, accessed April 26, 2021, https://www.blueletterbible.org/faq/don_stewart/don_stewart_303.cfm.

10. Don Stewart, "What Is Progressive Revelation?," *Blue Letter Bible*, accessed April 26, 2021, https://www.blueletterbible.org/faq/don_stewart/don_stewart_1203.cfm.

11. Don Stewart, "What Is Christian Theology?," *Blue Letter Bible*, accessed April 26, 2021, https://www.blueletterbible.org/Comm/stewart_don/faq/bible-basics/question1-what-is-christian-theology.cfm.

12. BibleStudyTools, s.v. "Theophany," accessed April 26, 2021, https://www.biblestudytools.com/dictionary/theophany.

Heresies

1. *Merriam-Webster*, s.v. "Arianism," accessed April 26, 2021, https://www.merriam-webster.com/dictionary/arianism.

2. *Merriam-Webster*, s.v. "Docetism," accessed April 26, 2021, https://www.merriam-webster.com/dictionary/Docetism.

3. *Merriam-Webster*, s.v. "gnosticism," accessed April 26, 2021, https://www.merriam-webster.com/dictionary/gnosticism.

4. *Merriam-Webster*, s.v. "henotheism," accessed April 26, 2021, https://www.merriam-webster.com/dictionary/henotheism.

5. *Merriam-Webster*, s.v. "modalism," accessed April 26, 2021, https://www.merriam-webster.com/dictionary/modalism.

6. *Merriam-Webster*, s.v. "monarchianism," accessed April 26, 2021, https://www.mcrriam-webster.com/dictionary/monarchianism.

7. *Merriam-Webster*, s.v. "monophysitism," accessed April 26, 2021, https://www.merriam-webster.com/dictionary/monophysitism.

8. *Merriam-Webster*, s.v. "nestorianism," accessed April 26, 2021, https://www.merriam-webster.com/dictionary/nestorianism.

9. *Merriam-Webster*, s.v. "polytheism," accessed April 26, 2021, https://www.merriam-webster.com/dictionary/polytheism.

10. *Merriam-Webster*, s.v. "subordinationism," accessed April 26, 2021, https://www.merriam-webster.com/dictionary/subordinationism.

11. *Merriam-Webster*, s.v. "tritheism," accessed April 26, 2021, https://www.merriam-webster.com/dictionary/tritheism.

12. *Merriam-Webster*, s.v. "unitarianism," accessed April 26, 2021, https://www.merriam-webster.com/dictionary/unitarianism.

Athanasian Creed

1. R. C. Sproul, "The Athanasian Creed," accessed September 28, 2022, https://www.ligonier.org/learn/articles/athanasian-creed.

2. "Athanasian Creed," CRCNA, accessed April 23, 2021, https://www.crcna.org/welcome/beliefs/creeds/athanasian-creed.

Want to explore

THE TRINITY

as a Bible study?

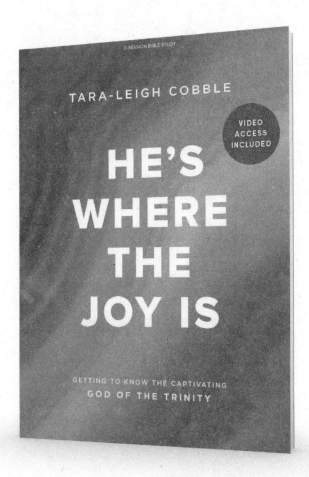

Check out Tara-Leigh Cobble's
parallel study, *He's Where the Joy Is.*